The Psychic Search

ii

Published by Guy Gannett Publishing Co., 390 Congress Street,
Portland, Maine 04101, August, 1981

First edition printed in the United States of America by
KJ Printing, Augusta, Maine 04330, August, 1981

Library of Congress Catalog Card # 81-81542

ISBN # 0-930096-22-3 — Hardcover Edition
ISBN # 0-930096-16-9 — Softcover Edition

Shirley Harrison

Lynn Franklin

The Psychic Search

By
Shirley Harrison
and
Lynn Franklin

Guy Gannett Publishing Co.

 PORTLAND / MAINE

Dedication

For my children, for Dorothy Morse Dickinson and for "Mr. Alan", and to all those wherever they are, whomever they are, who also are exploring the many mysteries of parapsychology and ESP and pursuing their own psychic searches.

Acknowledgments

An editor's role is not usually credited on the cover of a book and neither is it likely to be mentioned inside it. And yet, the fact is that no investigative reporter develops a book length documentary alone. Consequently, I want to thank Allan Swenson, our editor and overall director, as Shirley Harrison and I collaborated with official sources and principals to produce this book.

Special appreciation must also be expressed to all those police, government and private sources who gave freely of their valuable time to assist in the documentation of this book. These include Ernest Bracy of the FAA, Chief of Police Frank Stevens, and Bruce Publicover. Without their assistance, I could not have documented the uncanny abilities of this rare person, my psychic friend and co-author, Shirley Harrison.

Foreword and Forewarning

I've seen crystal ball gazers and tea leaf readers at numerous county fairs across America, as we all have. True psychics however, have truly amazed me.

So, when writer Lynn Franklin proposed this book, my first reaction was disbelief. It was not the typical Gannett book. However, his abiding faith, as an admitted skeptic, in this person, Shirley Harrison, provoked my curiosity. I agreed to look at a detailed outline. With a proviso. All cases he planned to include in the manuscript must be fully and factually authenticated and verified by official sources. That meant, signed affidavits or letters from police chiefs, FAA officials, private detectives, and all key participants in this psychic phenomenon that seemed to be Shirley Harrison.

When the first part of this book, the documented case histories arrived, I read them thoroughly and thoughtfully. They were astonishing, if real. Before Lynn could object, I picked up the phone and called every one of the principals involved. The experience was awesome.

Not only did they affirm the incredible and unexplainable things Shirley had done, they all indicated that they had become believers in ESP and psychic powers in the process. For a book editor who must remain a skeptic, that was revealing and remarkable.

Since, as the editor-in-chief of our Book Division, I am responsible for the factual content and quality of our books, I was still hesitant to publish a book by and about a psychic. So, I picked several names out of my own past on two different occasions when Shirley was in my office. In effect, I tested her at a moments notice, unannounced. On both those occasions she raised goose bumps on my arms. The information she revealed about those people and their life could not have been known to Shirley. Both were intelligence operatives I had known, respected and worked with years before. Yet Shirley, precisely and with uncanny accuracy, detailed parts of their lives that their wives probably did not know. That was unnerving. And, it helped convince me that this unexplainable thing called psychic power is indeed a reality, possessed in surprising degree by one Shirley Harrison.

Before this book was published, orders began to pour in for it. As it went to press, thousands of copies had been presold. Evidently, as word seeped out that the book was imminent, many others wish to discover more about Shirley Harrison and her powers.

During the many months this book has been in preparation, it became apparent that there are many other equally bizarre and exciting stories in the life of Shirley Harrison. They came to light, often in casual conversation over coffee at the end of a long day. Consequently, I asked Shirley to begin a sequel. She has. It will involve her work with police authorities in the investigation of crimes. More importantly, she is also presently working with a respected leading midwestern university on precisely this type of study. Where that book will lead is anyone's guess. Perhaps to a dead end. One thing is certain. If it follows the pattern of this first book, it may well prove even more compelling than such supernatural writers as Stephen King could ever dream up. For one important reason. Shirley's experiences are real. Of that there is no longer any doubt.

Allan A. Swenson
Editor-in-Chief
Guy Gannett Books

A Step Beyond

This book is a biography of Shirley Harrison, the true story of an astounding psychic. It also is, in large part, an autobiography by Shirley Harrison; her vivid recollections and reflections of her amazing psychic powers from the first days she became aware that somehow, for some reason, she had abilities unlike those around her.

There is a third dimension to this book, a step beyond the point where other books about psychics end. It is the authentication, the verification and documentation from those with whom Shirley Harrison has worked. These trained observers, police and sheriff's deputies, Federal Aviation Administration officials and others in authority, attest to the truth and the facts of what Shirley Harrison has done with her psychic powers.

Woven together, this investigative biography, her own autobiography and the documentation, provide both an over-all perspective of an amazing person and personality; and an inner view of a truly remarkable human being: Shirley Harrison, a rare psychic sensitive.

Psychics, those unique people who have a rare degree of extraordinary power to perceive things that others cannot see or know, have another power. They astound, fascinate and mystify people who know them.

Headlines and stories in newspapers periodically tell about a psychic here, another there, who has displayed his or her unusual powers in newsmaking ways. There have been books written about and by some psychics. They make good reading, but often seem to leave much unproved. These are stories about what the psychics themselves have said, without much evidence to support what they claim to have done.

Being a natural skeptic, part cynic, as well as a trained investigative reporter, I have read many of these reports and books. They're fun reading, but I remained a skeptic, disbelieving the stories, or at least much of them, until I could be convinced otherwise.

Among all the stories I had read and heard, that of one woman stood alone as perhaps more credible than all the others. She was Shirley Harrison, an unassuming mother of six children in West Buxton, Maine. I had met Shirley only once and was both impressed and intrigued by her and by what she claimed to have done with her psychic powers. It occurred to me that perhaps her life and "subtle craft" were worth investigating further by some interviews with her. That sounded easy. I was not prepared for the direction our meeting took, nor for the time that I was intrigued to invest. From that initial interview session, I realized that there was much more to this person than I originally had expected. That meeting, and hundreds of subsequent hours, led me to this book.

All my training from editors, from fellow investigative reporters and writers, taught me to dig behind supposed facts in search of documentation, verification, corroboration; from all available sources. Naturally, I wanted my sources to verify the clear and convincing accounts Shirley Harrison herself told me of her parapsychological experiences. But I was not prepared for such clear verification, often right on target.

More importantly, neither was I prepared to learn so many more real facts beyond those which Shirley herself related during the ensuing months of tape recorded conversations. Despite my best efforts at reserve and self-control, I found myself astounded and confounded.

What was even more astounding was that my sources, all of whom had training that would tend to make them astute, reliable observers, reported that they sometimes felt empowered by Shirley's paranormal feats which they had witnessed firsthand. Half-hour appointments with these sources ran into three and four hour interviews in depth. In some cases, hardboiled skeptics had become, it appeared, persuaded believers.

Among them I found sheriffs and their deputies, detectives, pharmacists, doctors, biologists and ministers. I interviewed and transcribed my notes and tapes. I found stories so strange, so incredible, that I returned to my sources to have the pages of my transcripts signed and thus further affirmed. You will find these revealing firsthand affidavits of psychic phenomenon in this book.

In accepting this assignment, I warned my editor that I anticipated exposing distortions, contradictions, coverups, and the ingenious reconstruction of events in the revealing light of clear 20-20 hindsight. I intended to document these tales as factually as the attested truth, if that should be the case.

Shirley Harrison agreed to be interviewed with that understanding clearly emphasized. Instead of reacting defensively, she endorsed my credo. Consequently, our working arrangement was a friendly, investigative, documented, shared authorship. It was a relationship not without argument and heated exchange. At times, my probing questions ignited fire in her response, especially when my questions seemed accusative.

In the face of acclaim and denial alike, Shirley's attitude remained unassuming and natural. She fielded even the most malicious criticism with the unfailing sense of humor of a lady. She has spoken on her subject across the country. She has been invited to lecture by such research scientists as those working at the Menninger Foundation, the Maimonedes Medical Center, and the American Institute for Psychical Research. Yet, except for a few classes in psychology and music at the University of Maine, her formal education does not go beyond the first year at Ricker College in her home county of Aroostook, Maine. Primarily, Shirley has gained her education and her knowledge naturally, and through her own self-taught techniques.

Yet, through the years, she has learned much from life and has much to teach. What she has done and discovered, about herself and about psychic phenomena, are indeed remarkable.

Some basic facts about Shirley Harrison, psychic, are in order as background, a preface to a clearer understanding of this book and of Shirley herself.

It is an established fact that Shirley Harrison, mother of six children, daughter of a Maine hunting and fishing guide and a country schoolteacher, has pinpointed the location of bodies sought by police when some of the most intensive searches in New England criminal history proved un-rewarding.

It is an established fact that Shirley Harrison, lecturing before a national conference of psychologists in Manhattan, predicted the location and the occupation of the next victim of the notorious Boston Strangler.

It is a fact that Shirley has located downed airplanes with such unexplained accuracy that Federal Aviation Administration officials now consult her when they are unable to find overdue aircraft.

There are many other facts that have been established by respected authorities attesting to the psychic powers of Shirley Harrison. But, none of these facts, all carefully brought together and examined, can add up to an explanation of *how* she does what she does.

Any writer, especially an investigative reporter, digging into the life story of a person such as Shirley Harrison, must assume that the burden of proof lies on his shoulders. She agreed to that honest, forthright approach. "The more strange the phenomenon," counseled Shirley, "the greater the documentation needed and the greater the need for under-statement."

While writing this book, I have held my beliefs in abeyance. What we needed, I knew, were observed facts. I adopted the credo of my college tutor, Henry Grattan: "The job of the explorer is to make a record of what he finds and to leave the conclusions to those who come later."

The problem of documenting Shirley Harrison's abilities was compounded when I confronted balky elected officials; sheriffs, district attorneys and career detectives. Usually, I had in hand letters and notes attesting to the fact that these people had solicited Shirley Harrison for information. Often this involved murders, missing persons, robberies. Yet, even when Shirley's information proved accurate, the official some-times denied publicly that he had sought the advice of a psychic sensitive.

For example, the district attorney of Boston said he, "pre-ferred computers to psychic sensitives," after one of the most hideous crimes in the history of Boston was carried out as Shirley had predicted. However, I had learned that his detec-tives had paid Shirley's transportation to Boston, had registered her in a hotel under an alias, had questioned her for long exhausting hours. Still, the DA refused to admit to any association with her.

The editor of a newspaper in Aroostook, Shirley's own home county, denied categorically that Shirley had pinpointed the body of a missing child on a farm outside his town. Yet, the evidence was overwhelming. Her revelation had been witnessed by dozens of conventioners attending a seminar which Shirley had been addressing. It was attested to by a Deputy Secretary of State. Shirley had predicted a child had been "struck too hard on the head," and that he was "on the Cheney place, under a huge log in water." That was in fact how the child had been killed and where his body was eventually found!

There were other cases in which sources hesitated to admit that they had worked with, much less used, the information provided by a psychic sensitive.

Fortunately, during the many months of research for this book, I was able to establish a rapport with my shy sources. Eventually, I was able to gain their confidence and elicit the facts of each case to my own satisfaction; and more importantly, to my editor's satisfaction.

During our work together, Shirley had told me that many people had telephoned her over the years to request that she use her psychic abilities to help them. On one occasion, an attorney friend jokingly asked Shirley whether there might not be a law against using psychic powers. At the time, Shirley dismissed the idea that what she was doing might somehow be illegal. After all, from her point of view, using her psychic powers was part of her own independent research, probing for ways to put her unique abilities to productive use. Many officials, from deputy sheriffs to game wardens, had requested her assistance.

"What could be illegal about what I do?" she asked herself.

On a hunch that the use of psychic sensitivity might actually be illegal in Maine, her home state, I sent a query to the State Law Library in Augusta.

The reply was prompt, and surprising.

The "subtle craft" indeed was illegal in Maine until 1971. An old "blue law" found in Maine Revised Statutes Annotated 17—3758 reads: ". . . persons using any subtle craft . . . pretending to have knowledge of physiognomy, palmistry, to tell destinies or fortunes, or to discover lost or stolen goods . . . may on complaint under oath before the District Court . . . be committed to jail or to the house of correction in the town where the person belongs or is found, for a term of not more than 90 days."

It appears that the story I was tracking, documenting and developing was not only illegal in Maine prior to 1971, but also currently taboo in the culture of New England. Maine is not unique in this way. Many people, especially public officials, frown on the use of psychics in the course of investigations. On the one hand, I sympathized with the reluctance of some people among my sources to admit their apparently intimate beliefs, especially to a persistently intruding reporter and author. On the other hand, I suspected they were denying their knowledge of the irrational and uncanny because, in every case, I had evidence that they had factual knowledge of the psychic powers of Shirley Harrison.

During the course of my investigations and interviews, it appeared that witnesses seemed to draw spiritual strength from Shirley. Sometimes, it was strongly apparent when they did relate their incredible story of her powers, that they seemed to be purging themselves of occult, somehow forbidden knowledge. It would seem that the old mores of Puritan New England still inhibit free inquiry into this "subtle craft."

Among the many strange discoveries I made while preparing this book, perhaps an episode with a group of Indians adds another dimension to this "subtle craft."

In fact, this may be one of the most meaningful tributes ever paid to a psychic sensitive in our culture. It was bestowed upon Shirley Harrison by her Maine neighbors, the Penobscot Indians.

A formal delegation, dressed in soft white leather, embossed and braided with sacred circles, arrived at Shirley's door in West Buxton one evening.

Shirley greeted them, saying, "I felt you were coming."

"Of course you did," said White Flower, the leader of the group. "We sent you a message that we were coming to you. We were drumming you."

"You are one of us," said White Flower. She presented Shirley with a carved ceremonial medicine stick and an amulet to make her welcome among Indians anywhere in America and Canada. And then White Flower extended an invitation which affected the psychic deeply. She invited Shirley to the Penobscot annual rite in which the spirits of the dead are consulted about the plans of the tribe for the coming year.

"They are a psychic sensitive people," Shirley explains.

And so, perhaps the "subtle craft" has been practiced in Maine, New England and America for a very long time indeed.

For all these diverse sources, I transcribed hours of tape recorded interviews, precisely following every word Shirley and my other sources had said for accuracy. Listening to their verifications, the sometimes stunned, always revealing nuances of their voices on tape as they retold the story and answered questions, my first instincts were reaffirmed. Shirley Harrison was, and is, an extraordinary woman possessed of special, unique powers.

From those long months of detailed research, and with the help of Shirley Harrison, who added other recollections as this manuscript developed, has come this book.

Many people have claimed ESP and psychic powers. Many have told of strange and eerie events in their lives. This book goes beyond those who merely claim what they have done or seen or heard. This book verifies from extensive research and documented facts that Shirley Harrison, the sensitive, has actually done what she claims to have done. In this significant regard it is demonstrably different from all previous books about psychic sensitives.

Despite this proof of her extraordinary and unusual powers, one fact cannot be explained. Neither Shirley Harrison nor I can explain how she does what she does. There is no doubt remaining about what she has accomplished. The people who know her and who have worked with Shirley have verified and proved their case, and hers.

Lynn Franklin
Portland, Maine
June, 1981

The General's Missing Daughter

During my early research into what I soon discovered was the astounding story of Shirley Harrison, I had assembled notes about a variety of unusual — and incredible — cases in which she was said to have played an all-important role. These cases included a suicide, a cross-country kidnapping, a lost aircraft search, a matter of missing jewelry and a murdered newspaper carrier. Each case was to prove different as I investigated it, and yet each case seemed to amplify in my mind the growing realization that Shirley Harrison's were truly amazing psychic powers. Naturally, I wanted to learn more as I began to suspect that further detailed checking might actually confirm the truth of Shirley Harrison's clairvoyance in these matters.

One case in particular, that of the disappearance of the daughter of an Army general, demanded my immediate attention. The story had made national headlines, yes, but more important to my search was the fact that veteran officials whom I respected were available to answer my questions. I resolved to make these questions blunt and probing. I did not solicit the polite answers of public officials anxious to tell me what they thought I wanted to hear. I needed hard facts to verify or disprove what Shirley Harrison had told me she had done.

In this case of the daughter of the general, Shirley claimed to have actually pinpointed the location of the child. I admit that I doubted very much if the police chief I intended to interview would commit himself to verification or denial of this uncanny claim. Instead, I expected him to avoid personal involvement by referring me to the cold, matter-of-fact, police records of the matter. In any case, this seemed the logical first step if I were to track down and develop the story of Shirley Harrison. What I learned here could prove or disprove her story of psychic powers.

It was on August 9th, 1970, that Mary Catherine Olenchuk, the 13-year-old, vivacious, freckled and blue-eyed daughter of an Army brigadier general, disappeared a few blocks from her Ogunquit summer home.

Apparently she left her family on the beach at 4 p.m. She returned to their cottage on nearby Shore Road. There she changed into faded pink shorts and a white T-shirt with Yokomiko Andrews AFB stenciled on the front. She hung her bathing suit on the line where it was found that evening. She borrowed a neighbor's bicycle and rode into town. There she bought a New York Times, a pack of gum and some candy.

Two employees at the nearby Marginal Way House recognized her and waved. The time was 4:30 p.m. A guest at The Lookout Hotel came forward the following day and reported that she had seen Mary Catherine talking to a dark-haired man, about 30, in a maroon car. The car had a scratched hood and it was parked at the curb in front of the hotel. Both the child and the man seemed to be smiling, she said. She admitted she had turned away, if only briefly, from the window. When she turned back, Mary Catherine was in the car headed in the direction of Israel's Head. The guest could not recall the make of the car nor its license number.

Later, the bicycle was found neatly parked in an alcove of the hotel.

August 9th in 1970 was a Sunday, and at 7:15 p.m. Mrs. Olenchuk telephoned the Ogunquit police to report that her daughter had not come home. At 8:30 p.m. she went in person to the station to ask that the State Police use their wider resources to help find her daughter.

A missing persons teletype was relayed along the Eastern Seaboard. By midnight, a detailed description of Mary Catherine had been transmitted nationwide. Meanwhile, the local police had summoned volunteer firemen into the search which lasted until 5 a.m. Monday.

By noon, Mary Catherine's father, Brig. General Peter G. Olenchuk, had arrived at Pease Air Force Base in nearby New Hampshire. He had flown in from Edgewater Arsenal, Maryland, where he was temporarily assigned. General Olenchuk was commander of the Army Ammunition Supply Agency at Joliet, Illinois.

The general was also in charge of a controversial cross-country shipment of nerve gas that was to be buried at sea several hundred miles off Cape Kennedy, Florida. There had been several public protests against burying the gas at sea. The possibility that Mary Catherine had been abducted in reprisal against the general brought FBI agents from Portland and Boston into the search.

Interviews with Mary Catherine's family revealed nothing in her background to indicate that she might disappear on her own.

"Mary is 13 trying hard to be 14," General Olenchuk told newspeople. "She is very much interested in fishing . . . quite talented . . . a very warm personality . . . She has striking auburn hair similar in color to her Irish setter's . . . a cheerful smile. She's a little shy and reserved, but very friendly."

Late Wednesday afternoon an army helicopter patrolled the coast from Portsmouth, New Hampshire, to Old Orchard Beach, Maine.

Police logged calls describing maroon cars at the rate of one every 20 seconds. Extra telephones were installed at the police station and manned by deputies around the clock.

Police barricades blocked travellers. All were questioned, but no clues were forthcoming.

Shirley Harrison remembers that it was in the evening of August 13th when she was at home in West Buxton about thirty miles from Ogunquit, that her phone rang and an elderly lady introduced herself as the aunt of Mary Catherine Olenchuk. The aunt asked Shirley to help find Mary Catherine and expressed confidence in Shirley.

"I can't promise success," said Shirley. "But I will try."

"I understand," said the elderly voice. "God bless you."

"Incidentally," said Shirley. "I have an unlisted telephone How did you get my number?"

"The FBI is working with us," said the aunt. "Their agent told me that officially he could not consult a psychic sensitive, but off the record, he gave me your number."

Nothing in Shirley's life was more sacred than the well-being of her children, and, as an extension, of all children. Shirley remembers that she went immediately into her living room and sat before the piano. There she resolved to banish whatever doubts she felt about her powers, and to learn what she could.

"I doubted my powers at that time," remembered Shirley.

Yet, I knew that time and again, before conventions of

academics, research scientists — obdurate skeptics and ardent believers — she had been able to identify hidden objects, to name names, to describe residences, recite identifying numbers and addresses. She had done this countless times as scientists had confirmed. Yet she was inevitably amazed when her information proved accurate.

"Sometimes," she explains, "I just seem to know."

I had learned from her twins that Shirley had told them the precise number of paces from a tree and in what direction they would find their baseball so often it had become part of their game.

I knew she had told Federal Aviation Administration station chiefs throughout New England the location of lost airplanes, sometimes far off course. She had done this so often the FAA routinely called her when an aircraft was reported lost.

I had learned that at the time of the Olenchuk case, and in fact, all of her adult life, she had somehow known when dear friends were in trouble. Often she would phone them, I learned, only to discover they had, indeed, been sick, in the hospital, or experiencing the problem she envisioned.

On the night of this case, after receiving the phone call, Shirley remembers that seated at her piano, she centered her consciousness on Mary Catherine Olenchuk. The child's location, Shirley remembers, would be like a piece of music she was to compose that night. She concentrated, in expectation of the succeeding notes, a score she had never seen and, if she were to save the child, a score she must learn within a few hours.

It was after 10 o'clock when she finally dialed the number the aunt had given her.

Shirley remembers that she spent 20 concentrated minutes intently focussing her consciousness on the little girl.

"I thought, I concentrated to myself, 'Where is she?' The answer came to me: 'Kennebunk.'

"I asked myself, 'What is her situation? How is she?' I received the feeling, like an answer to my own question, that she was dead, 'hanged by a rope.' I hoped in my heart that this was not true. I prayed that the girl was still alive, and that somehow we could find her alive and well.

"So, once again, I concentrated this time even more intently. I became so intense that my mind almost hurt. I asked myself questions: 'Where is she in Kennebunk? Where should we look?' Kennebunk is a big place.

"Then, suddenly," remembers Shirley, "I received an impression of an unpainted building, of a building on the estate of a wealthy person. I saw three roads coming together where they form a perfect Y, and a place nearby, a business owned by a person named Pillsbury.

"On that property, on the estate, I saw hundreds of little trees like a tree nursery."

Shirley remembers that she saw other things, frightening things that she did not want to contemplate. But she continued to concentrate, to focus her psychic energy into the search for the little girl.

When she was finished, she turned to her husband who had been taking notes of what images and impressions came to her mind as she described them.

Then, reading the notes herself, she called the aunt and related what she had envisioned.

The aunt thanked her. We can only speculate that the aunt relayed this information when she called Frank Stevens at the Kennebunk Police Department.

Frank Stevens' office in the cinderblock basement of the Kennebunk Police Station resembled a bunker. Its narrow windows afforded a pavement level view of patrol car tires in the station lot. His walls held certificates of completion of police academy curriculums, honorary memberships in fraternal orders of police chiefs, J. Edgar Hoover awards.

Stevens was a chunky 210 pounds. He was 54. He had come back home after sailing five times across the Atlantic and once around the world. "That was in '41 on the SS Waxhaws," said Frank, "a T-2 ship hauling high octane gas. I was a gunner."

When he got home to where his ancestors had farmed and traded and built ships and gone to sea, Frank enlisted in the police force. After ten years — "How do you break up a street fight? Mostly with your head!" — he made chief. That was in '58. Since then he'd been reappointed by nine town managers. Once he was town manager himself.

Frank is outspoken with little regard for subtleties or niceties. He uses rough language, but with a certain charm which nullifies criticism. He speaks his mind bluntly and spontaneously. He is sometimes flamboyant. Yet he is sensitive.

During the Olenchuk case, Stevens remembers, a police radio on his desk monitored 13 cruisers. There was an intercom to the dispatcher and a telephone. There was an FM radio crooning music. It soothed a constant stomach pain Frank was determined to cure himself. He kept a quart of Maalox in the top drawer of his desk and he swigged the white, chalky, medication in secret at the rate of two bottles a week, but it didn't help much.

He had been feeling wrenching, stabbing, stomach pains when the aunt of Mary Catherine Olenchuk called that morning. It was the general's sister. She notified Frank that she was soliciting a psychic sensitive, a Mrs. Harrison of West Buxton. She was waiting for her call.

"Jeeeeeeeeesus," he said, "that psychic stuff gives me the creeps."

Shirley Harrison: A scenario came back to him word for word — a feat of recollection he developed in 35 years as a police officer.

It was a TV show, Channel 13 out of Portland, early in the summer. She was a parapsychologist, president of a psychical research society. She seemed intelligent, in Frank's opinion. She admitted mistakes, admitted she was often wrong, often confused.

Frank's memory returned to that TV show. Shirley Harrison had said that ESP wasn't something she could do on demand just anytime. Frank Stevens remembered that show vividly.

The MC, Harry Marble, had said, "Mrs. Harrison, we have prepared a test for your powers. Would you identify what is in this envelope?"

Frank had decided it was rigged.

"I can't promise anything," Shirley had replied.

"You're not kidding," Stevens had thought.

"But, I'll try," she added. The MC handed her an envelope. She must have looked directly at the red light over the unwinking eye of the video camera lens because she seemed to gaze at Frank on his living room sofa and said. "This is a piece of wire from the Berlin Wall!"

"Bull!" Stevens had said.

The MC was on screen, slumping in his chair.

Then Harry Marble had said hurriedly, "Mrs. Harrison has identified the object. Our purpose was to test her psychic powers which are widely acclaimed. Mrs. Harrison could not possibly have known in any normal way what is concealed in this envelope. The object is a piece of wire brought back by our station manager from his recent trip to West Germany. And it actually is a piece of the Berlin Wall!"

"That was Shirley Harrison," mused Stevens. "That was showbusiness, too."

He remembered another case in which Shirley had been right; the time she told State Police Chief of Homicide, Camille Carrier, that the body of a 12-year-old newsboy, Cyrus Everett, was lying in water under something heavy on the "Cheney place" outside Fort Fairfield, 300 miles north.

"That's where they found the boy in the spring. Not only that," remembered Frank, "she told Carrier that a man 'who knows a great deal in this matter' owns a pickup truck. She described his house and his occupation and his address. 'You'd better question him soon,' she had warned Carrier, 'because he plans to do away with himself.' "

Before Carrier could check out her premonition, he received a report that one of the prime witnesses in the case was found dead from carbon monoxide poisoning in the cab of his pickup truck.

Frank Stevens wondered how much of his time she would require before the general's sister let him off the hook.

The police search had not found Mary Catherine that week or that day or that night. After receiving Shirley's information from the aunt, Frank remembers that he sat deep in thought

The dispatcher had looked at him as if to ask if he was really working on this case or not? There were still no leads, nothing to report that morning; nothing that Frank was willing to report, anyway.

He had road blocks in position. People driving to work or to the beach were being stopped two or even three times for questioning. Anybody who had a maroon car better know where it was after 4 p.m. that Sunday. There were a lot of scared people in Kennebunk and Ogunquit.

"They blamed me for not doing the impossible, if you understand me," said Frank.

Frank said he had to decide right then, with Shirley's information in hand, whether to believe her story or not. In order to use her information, he said, he had to screen everything she had said, and reject what he thought was doubtful. Either that, or he had to follow up on everything.

Frank remembers that he reviewed her information in his mind. "Where three roads come together," she had said. "Look for a place in Kennebunk. The road forms a perfect Y. Nearby is a business owned by somebody named Pillsbury. An old estate," she had said. "The building is unpainted. There is a tree nursery on the estate."

"I knew," said Frank, "there was an unpainted building on the Parson's Estate. It was an old shingled barn. All the other buildings on that estate were painted. That meant the old barn. It was something certain in my mind . . ."

But Frank had searched that barn; twice, in fact, and recently. The second time was on the day Mary Catherine's aunt called saying she had been talking to Shirley Harrison. The barn was the kind of place your imagination would tell you there might be something. Kids like old barns. Hippies like old barns. There was hay and machinery in it, abandoned 50 years before.

Frank screened her information. "I knew a Pillsbury who lived on Brown Street and ran a plumbing and heating business out of his yard. But I couldn't think of a perfect Y nearby. There was a Y, but it was a mile off. There was a diamond in town. They always called it that. If that was what she meant, why didn't she call it a diamond? I couldn't place a tree nursery on the Parson's Estate.

"Anyway," said Frank, "I told one of my officers to check out the unpainted barn on the Parson's Estate.

"He reminded me that I had already checked it out. Twice! Made me feel like I was losing my grip.

"I know," I said. "Check it again."

That was an order.

That day was hot, 100 degrees, like they'd been having all summer. Frank's officer called in to headquarters about 11 a.m. He said he and the caretaker had found the body. It was down two feet in the hay in that unpainted barn on the Parson's Estate.

"I don't think of myself as excitable," said Frank, "but I hit the siren switch on the cruiser. I could hear another siren, then another. The state troopers were monitoring, coming in also."

He drove on the grass beside the officer's cruiser. The

first thing he noticed was a smell. It was a lot stronger than when he searched the place five days before. At that time he had thought it was birds. He went in and there was his officer and the caretaker.

"Inside the smell was worse than you can imagine," said Frank, "unless you've been around human remains. It's something you have to experience."

It was just a slip of a body. There was nothing around her neck that he could see. She was in her T-shirt, "something-or-other AFB on it," and her shorts.

"I've been doing this work a long time," said Frank, "and I've got used to things, but I'll tell you I broke down."

He went out to the cruiser and ordered the barn cordoned off. He told the dispatcher to call the coroner. He told her to call somebody else as well; Shirley Harrison.

"What I wanted to do," said Frank, "was thank her. If I had any doubt about Shirley Harrison when I first heard of her, I was 95 percent more certain now. I don't know if she can do it every time. Neither does she. But she did it this time."

From Shirley's recollections and from Frank Stevens' confirmation of them, I knew that Shirley had actually described where the body was. "The proof is we found it," said Frank. "It was where she said it was. It was there! Part of her description was right down to a T, close enough to back up everything she said."

A few more factors fell into place after that. One of them was that Shirley had mentioned a rope. The first autopsy didn't reveal a rope, but the second autopsy revealed a piece of lobster warp in the neck.

"So to my mind at the time," said Frank, "Shirley was correct twice. It wasn't until two years later that I realized she had been right more often than just twice."

Frank Stevens turned to a fresh page on his clipboard and wrote down the following just like algebra. He wrote: KNOWN, 1, Unpainted barn on the Parson's Estate. 2, Rope, Strangled, Dead. 3, Pillsbury Plumbing and Heating Company. 4, Perfect Y in the road. 5, Tree nursery.

"I didn't know the tree nursery was a known," said Frank, "until several years after the murder. As a matter of fact, they have been selling Christmas trees from it four or five years now. It's on the Parson's Estate, but at the time we found the body, it was several acres of seedlings not as high as the grass around it. But it was there and it was what she said it was."

Then Frank spread out a map of York County and laid it beside his clipboard. He made an X over a perfect Y in the road about a mile and a half out of town. He made an X over the Pillsbury Plumbing and Heating Company and another X over the unpainted barn site and the Christmas tree nursery.

The Xs were in line leading down Brown Street to the site of the unpainted barn. But they were not close by — not unless you were viewing the scene as part of the entire county.

"Close by, to me," said Frank, "means a quarter mile at the most. But I live in Kennebunk. To an outsider, a person viewing Kennebunk as a small part of York County or as an even smaller part of Southern Maine, close by could mean many miles; up to five, I'd say.

"I'm still trying to understand Shirley Harrison," said Frank. "What she did was accurate, but she seems to see from a different perspective in relation to distance."

As an investigative reporter, I had learned that few observers are more objective than a trained police officer of many years experience. Frank Stevens' verification of my interview was solid evidence that Shirley had pinpointed the unpainted barn in the right area and that Shirley had predicted the child had been strangled. She had been correct far beyond any random guessing.

Realizing this, I wanted to know more, much more. I wanted to know what it was like to be a psychic sensitive such as Shirley Harrison. I wanted to seek out those with whom she had worked, to interview them, to transcribe our interviews and to return them for verification and clarification. I knew that only in this way, time consuming yet fascinating as it would be, could I develop facts and the true stories for this book.

So I returned to reinterview Chief Stevens. There was, as I suspected, more to be added to the story.

Shirley remembered that it was not until several weeks after the body had been found that Shirley finally met personally with Frank Stevens. Stevens had called Shirley and said in his characteristic manner, "We've got a murderer down here. The Olenchuk girl's murderer. Will you help us?"

"I would never point an accusing finger based on information I had gotten through ESP," Shirley had told the police chief. However, she would do what she could.

Shirley arrived at Frank's office the next day. She brought with her all of her notes on the case.

Shirley recalls that Frank Stevens' office was a dimly lit den in the rear of the station, and that the chief greeted her with a handshake. Her first impression was that he was a genial, likeable man, courteous, very strong and rugged looking, handsome in fact — but that he was very sick!

Impulsively, Shirley said to him, "Mr. Stevens, if I were you I'd throw away that bottle of Maalox you have in your desk drawer and get some good medical attention!"

Frank spooked, remembers Shirley.

"Don't do that in here!" he blurted. "Damn, that scares the hell out of me!"

And then he reached in the drawer and pulled out the bottle and showed it to Shirley.

In their ensuing search for the murderer, Shirley remembers that she told Frank to drive her along Route 9. She felt it was there she might locate the murderer. In fact, in her notes she had described houses, names on mailboxes. All of them were on Route 9.

Frank invited another police officer, recalled Shirley. It was Cecil Perkins, Chief of Police of Ogunquit. Shirley's husband at the time, Bill Cook, was also in the car. They drove along Route 9 all the way from Kennebunk to ten miles out of town.

"I made comments as to my intuitive feelings about each house," remembered Shirley. "One house affected me violently — a most positive feeling that it had a connection to the murder case. The effect was sinister and menacing. We were all a bit jumpy and nervous about it.

"The house was in my notes. I was seeing it for the first time and I actually got a feeling this was the house. There were scattered pieces of cars in the yard. There was a car pulled up under a tree. I had envisioned the murderer to be fond of working on cars, to be, in fact, preoccupied with them. I related the murderer to this house. I cannot deny," said Shirley, "the similarity in my mind between Charles Street near the jail in Boston where the Strangler murdered a woman, a murder I had foreseen, and this house on Route 9."

Frank's reaction was weird, too, said Shirley.

"Jeeeeeesus," said Frank, big and rugged as he was. "Let's get the hell off this road."

"Frank was forever telling me how I scared him to death."

No concrete evidence could be developed from Shirley's psychic feelings to provide sufficient evidence that linked any person to the murder, at least not sufficient proof to take a case to court.

The murderer of Mary Catherine Olenchuk is still at large, so far as we know, as this book goes to press. In the seasoned manner of a police officer, Frank stated matter-of-factly that Mary Catherine was dead. We couldn't bring her back.

Neither could he assure me that her murderer would not seek out Shirley Harrison. In fact, Shirley's safety was much on my mind.

"To some degree," said Frank, "the convicted criminal will forgive the police because we are only doing our duty. But he does not have forgiveness for a person on the outside, a person he might call an informer."

I had to agree that in a manner of speaking Shirley was an informer.

"If the murderer knew Shirley was steering police to him, I'd say, yes, her life is in danger. She must realize that," he added.

The attitude of criminals toward informers is one of ruthless revenge. So I knew that Shirley had risked her life in a desperate and vain attempt to save Mary Catherine Olenchuk. I was to learn this was not the first time she had risked her safety to help police apprehend the murderer of a child.

Lost Aircraft

Another mysterious and amazing aspect of Shirley Harrison's clairvoyance is her uncanny ability to focus in on lost aircraft and pinpoint their location. She has done this several times, not only in New England where she lives, but also in Florida and even, some sources say, in the jungles of Colombia.

This particular case, set in Maine, will provide some clues to the difficulty of such assignments. In order to understand the events of this lost aircraft case, one must envision the vast geography of the state of Maine itself. It is a region of contrasts, of bustling, modern cities on one hand and of immense tracts of commercial forest on the other.

Pilots flying across Maine draw straight lines across a chart of 20 mountains higher than 3,500 feet, of no less than 6,000 lakes and 5,000 streams and rivers; some flowing north into Canada, some south into the Gulf of Maine. The Maine coast itself extends along 3,000 miles, and offshore in swift tides lie more than 2,000 islands.

It is not only the terrain that is varied, but the weather is known to threaten fog one day and snow the next. Fifty-five days of fog a year is routine along the coast. In the vast interior it is reckoned by bushpilots to be a rare winter day, indeed, when there is not a snowsquall in sight, a menace to safe flying.

It is for these reasons that the Station Chiefs of the Federal Aviation Administration admonish pilots to be wary. It is easy to lose one's way. It has many times proved impossible to find downed pilots. Instances come to mind. There is Legassey, a legend in his lifetime of bushflying. Yes, they found him, but it was five years later and by chance. A warden pilot, late getting home, took a short cut over a mountain and spotted the aluminum gleam of "Chink's" ship on the side of a ridge at the edge of a pond. Chink was still in it.

There was Rasmussen. A six-week air search proved futile.

It was years later that a survey party on foot found him. His wingtip had caught a tree. Rasmussen's twisted wreck could not have been seen from the air, even if searchers had known where it was.

FAA officials do not claim to have a record of all the missing aircraft all over New England. In Maine, the FAA's Chief of Stations in Augusta, the state capitol, is Ernest L. Bracy, himself a veteran, world wandering aviator.

Understandably, the most thorough search must eventually be abandoned. The missing are more or less forgotten. Except, of course, by a few who despite all logic . . . truly persistent people, people who may be relatives, perhaps with a financial interest . . . continue the search on their own. Inevitably, eventually, they too give up the search and once again the wilderness has won.

The details described here are those of an actual case of an air search in which Shirley Harrison's psychic powers proved accurate. They are based, once again, on official records, in this case those of the FAA, and on press and first-person reports at the time. Also, in this case, the official air search had been called off as hopeless. I learned that it was renewed only after Shirley Harrison directed FAA officials to the crash site, a site she pinpointed by name.

It was on the night of Wednesday, September 9th, 1964, that Leta Haley, 43, and her husband, Everett Haley, 46, departed Houlton, Maine, bound for Beverly, Massachusetts, 285 miles south. Their aircraft was a Piper Tri-Pacer, single engine. Their mission was urgent. Haley's sister in Beverly was ill. And so Leta and Everett Haley took off at 10 p.m. They made routine contact with Bangor, 120 miles south along their course, as they flew over the area. The time was 11:32 p.m.

Their destination lay 200 miles further southwest. Range of the Tri-Pacer is not more than four and a half hours. At a ground speed of 100 mph, weather permitting, the couple should have arrived at Beverly at approximately 1:30 a.m. on Thursday. But they did not arrive. No radio message was reported along the way, with the exception of the 11:32 p.m. transmission to Bangor.

Alerted early Thursday, Bracy ordered a scan along the course the overdue pilot had plotted and filed with the authorities. Bracy was a friend and colleague of Everett Haley, who was chief of flight service for FAA at Houlton.

Bracy asked for help from Maine's Civil Air Patrol Wing. By noon, despite unstable weather, fifteen CAP pilots were flying low over the course Haley had filed. Complicating their mission was the red and cream color of the Tri-Pacer. It would blend with the dense foliage of trees now donning their red, orange and gold autumn colors.

Haley's course passed over the coast, one of the most indented, tidal races in North America.

By early afternoon Thursday, haze and rain, possibly related to Hurricane Donna then raging over Atlantic Beach in Florida, brought down a curtain of low visibility.

Coast Guard commanders offshore despaired of finding the Haleys in the murk, especially if they had crashed in coastal waters. Nevertheless, the CAP pilots flew 28 sorties by Thursday evening.

By Friday, the missing couple had been reported in the press and over radio and television. Rumors harassed the searchers. One pilot was sent to the distant Winterport area with a 12-man ground crew because a caller thought he heard an aircraft engine early Thursday. It might have been the Haleys.

Other tales came from as far away as Fitchburg, Mass. Finally, recognizing the futility of following up all rumors, Bracy bounded the search area with a rectangle on the aeronautic chart from Bangor west to Pittsfield, south to Augusta and east to the coast at Rockland.

Police checked small airports along the entire course from Houlton to Beverly. The Haleys had not been seen. They had not been heard.

A cold front moved into Maine Friday night. It cleared out the rain and provided excellent flying on Saturday.

More than 40 pilots volunteered their aircraft, their time and skill to search beginning Saturday at dawn. New Hampshire pilots searched the Fryeburg-Bethel area on the perimeter of the White Mountains. The Navy and the Air Force readied helicopters at Brunswick Naval Air Station and at Dow Air Force Field to retrieve the downed aviators should they be found.

State Police checked out still another rumor from Winterport that the Haleys had been heard in that area.

An Eastern Air Rescue team from Robins Air Force base in Macon, Georgia, 1,000 miles south, flew into New England on Saturday. Led by Major John E. Rapp, the team landed at Augusta. The pilots posed for photographs by the press. They flew sorties but they found no trace of the Piper Tri-Pacer.

After two days of flying from light to darkness, Major Rapp was dismayed by the immensity of the task. He gave up. He said that dense foliage made further aerial search useless and that a small plane, no matter what colors, could not be seen from the air among the shimmering reds and yellows of autumn foliage. The task is impossible, said Rapp. His team returned to Georgia.

By Monday, it had been five days since Everett and Leta Haley were reported overdue. But the Maine-based pilots persisted. They scanned along the vectors in Haley's flight plan from Kennebunk on the coast to Bangor in the interior. They flew into Houlton on the chance that Haley might have turned back.

At Augusta search headquarters the phones jangled with reports of sightings. Pilots were sent to scan around Frye Mountain in Unity, where, typically, "something" had been seen. A caller from Sheepscott Pond, right on course, reported an oil slick. Skin divers from Brunswick Naval Air Station dove in the area of the oil. They found an outboard motor.

Tracking down all the rumors proved time consuming and unrewarding.

It was agreed the search pilots had done their best. They had flown from light to dark, 200 feet over the forest 14 hours a day. Their searching had seemed to pull their eyes right out of their heads. They crawled out of their cockpits and into bunks where they slept like dead men. One thing was certain, the Haleys were not where the searchers thought they were.

Houlton to Beverly was quite a long way to search for something so camouflaged as a varicolored aircraft in autumn, particularly when there were no clues. For despite the increasing clamor of rumors, none had proved positive.

The search was canceled. The volunteer pilots, the FAA, the Navy, the Air Force and the police had done their utmost. The Tri-Pacer containing Everett and Leta Haley was now another missing aircraft somewhere in the vast wilderness or offshore.

Two days later Bracy recalls that a gentleman entered FAA's office at Augusta. He briefed Bracy. He said he was a brother of Leta Haley. He insisted that his sister would be found by psychic perception. His family was keen on readings, psychic readings. The grandmother especially foresaw success. He would consult a sensitive, Shirley Harrison of West Buxton.

"The next day," said Bracy, "the gentleman called me from Shirley Harrison's house. He said he must get back to Washington where he was an executive of the Boy Scouts. He actually presumed that Shirley Harrison was going to call me and tell me where to find Everett and Leta Haley. He was dogmatic about it," said Bracy. "He sounded persuaded."

This was not a source of information generally accepted by the public. It was understandably difficult to renew an aircraft search on the basis of it. But Bracy made a fair promise.

A short time later, just as predicted, Shirley Harrison called Bracy. She confirmed that, yes, a brother of Leta Haley had asked Shirley to find his sister. He had just departed for Washington.

Then Shirley told Bracy what she had learned from psychic concentration about the location of the Haley aircraft.

"I don't buy it," Bracy said. "You will have to go back to your sources, whatever they are, and refine your data. It's not good enough!"

And yet, Bracy recalls, Shirley did not speak in general. She did not repeat published information. If she had done so, Bracy would have thanked her for her concern and then discounted it, just as he would that of a survivor or loved one whose memory, muddied by exhaustion and anxiety, is often unreliable.

And it was also true that bits and pieces of Shirley's information, a name in particular, seemed somehow correct to Bracy. Some of her psychic feats were known to him. He would strive to distinguish fact from fancy by careful sensitive questioning. He asked Shirley to return to her source of knowledge, to confirm and reconfirm her information, and then to call him back at the FAA station in Augusta. He would remain in his office awaiting her call.

Shirley called back later that afternoon.

"I re-evaluated," said Shirley. "I finally fit that puzzle piece of a name into my information. I sent it back to my source and it returned to me repeatedly with an accompanying feeling of confidence."

It was only then that she had called Bracy a second time. She felt she had real information to offer him. She admitted candidly that she had hastily interpreted the name of a town. She now had another name of a town, a name similar in sound but distinctly different.

"I wonder if you will buy this one?" she asked. She said the Haleys had crashed "25 miles west of Goffstown, New Hampshire." She said the Haleys' aircraft was "in a sort of valley." It had "struck a tree on a mountain two-thirds of the way to the top." She said Everett and Leta Haley were "still in the aircraft."

She gave Bracy a number, "107," and then another number, "9-B." She told him which of the two Haleys had passed away first and she told him that one of them had "struggled to escape" from the aircraft.

This time Bracy was not only intrigued, he was astounded. He told Shirley that he would try to reopen the search, this time around Goffstown. It would take some persuading.

Goffstown, New Hampshire, lay 100 miles southwest of the search area Bracy and his team had enclosed. It was remote, indeed, from a likely crash site. It was 50 miles west of the Haleys' most direct route to Beverly.

No matter. Mindful of his promise and dismayed by the failure of airmen and police to find his friend despite an heroic search, Bracy called FAA's Concord, New Hampshire, Flight Service Station. It was the closest station to Goffstown.

Bracy's memory of some unusual coincidences throw side light on this story at this point.

"It is strange, but it is a fact," he said. "The chief at Concord that day was away and the acting chief of facility was an acquaintance of Shirley Harrison. He had visited at her house. His name was Batchelder. Maybe the chief himself would not have paid any attention to my report, but Batchelder," said Bracy, "told me he'd never argue with Shirley Harrison."

He told Bracy he would organize an official search for Everett and Leta Haley that weekend. Our basis for search, Batchelder told Bracy, will be that out in the Goffstown area somebody did see something that resembled an airplane.

Batchelder did, indeed, open the search with the National Guard in that area pinpointed by Shirley Harrison. But the aircraft was found by somebody who just happened to be in the woods.

"It is again oddly coincidental," said Bracy, "that those woods were part of a large estate managed by an intimate friend of the Haleys.

"The aircraft was within twenty-five miles of the town she had named," said Bracy. "I don't know how you could better have described it. The fact is it was the nearest town.

"I did see FAA photographs and analysis of the crash," Bracy added. "They further confirm Shirley's information. Everett and Leta Haley were, in fact, strapped in their seats. Leta Haley had, in fact, tried to open the door of the airplane and escape.

"The details she gave me," said Bracy, "were quite precise, quite accurate."

The search was over.

Reconsidering Shirley's information and its corroboration, Shirley's feat of clairvoyance seems all the more amazing. On a roadmap of New Hampshire, there is both a Gossville and a Goffstown. One of the mystery numbers in Shirley's information is 107. According to Bracy, it does not relate to any of the identifying numbers of the Haleys' airplane. Yet it is found on the map. It is the number of the highway around Gossville — not Goffstown — to the northeast. Shirley found this distortion intriguing.

"Another number in Shirley's information may relate to the Haley crash," said Bracy, "if we allow for distortion. That is the mysterious 9-B." The Haleys crashed directly on Vector 93. It is clearly marked on aviation charts of the region. Haley filed a flight plan before departing, a plan in which he named the vectors he would fly to his destination. Vector 93 was not one of them, yet that is where he was found. Once again, Shirley found that distortion intriguing. It did not erode her confidence in the pure knowledge which was her source. She blamed the distortion, if that were the case, on her conscious interpretation of the "silent music" of her powers.

A few more facets of this story are worth recounting. They reveal much about the controversial position of clairvoyance in our accepted modes of understanding things.

The ambivalent attitude of officialdom toward psychic perception, even when it proves rewarding, is again illustrated in Bracy's candid account of Shirley's amazing role in renewing the FAA's search.

"The information Shirley gave me," said Bracy, "probably did not become a matter of record. I doubt if anything of her role appeared in the official report of the accident."

"Not even the reason for initiating the search in that area?" I asked.

"No," answered Bracy. "It just happened to be a coincidence that two people walking in the woods found it at the same time in the same area."

"Were you searching the area that day because Shirley suggested you should be there?" I persisted.

"Yes," said Bracy, "but that was not the reason given for searching the area. The reason given was that somebody had seen something white on the side of a hill out that way."

"But she gave the information to you," I said.

"Yes," confirmed Bracy.

"And you passed it on to the chief in that area?"

"To the acting chief, yes," said Bracy.

"Did he or she act on it?"

"Yes."

There are other facets of this case of Shirley's clairvoyance in which destinies seemed to come together all in one place.

One such synchronous event is that the Haleys were found by two brothers not part of the search team who said that they normally went into those woods only once or twice a year to check a water source. They found the Haleys crashed against thick trees about two-thirds of the way up the mountain and at the edge of their trail. The brothers speculated that had the plane travelled any further, chances of seeing it from the trail would have been hopeless until after the fall foliage had fallen.

Another facet, again oddly coincidental, is that Leta Haley, nee Leta McNally of Dyer Brook, Aroostook County, Maine, was well known to Shirley Harrison. "We grew up together," Shirley remembered, "although we went to different schools. Leta's school was not ten miles from Island Falls."

"Would you call Shirley Harrison again in cases of missing aircraft?" I asked Bracy.

"Certainly," he said. "It might save lives."

Cross-Country Kidnapping

Across the continent, from Connecticut to California, Shirley's reputation spread rapidly as she became more and more active publicly with her psychic activities. She had earned respect of the police for her amazing accuracy in crime cases. At the same time, she was in demand not only for public performances, but also for seminars of scientists studying parapsychology. It was during this period that Shirley was tested by the famed William G. Roll at the Psychical Research Foundation in Durham, North Carolina.

Shirley was challenged. She learned that dedicated researchers into the amazing phenomenon of ESP were rare. Her public seemed to crave sensationalism. Nevertheless, she remained herself. Like an artist who believes utterly in her work, she did not betray her sensitive powers. She told what she knew. Indeed, Shirley was dedicated not to eerie ESP stories, but to a bewildering search for clues as to the source of her clairvoyant knowledge.

Perhaps it was because of her reputation for psychic integrity and research, that the following case was brought to Shirley. The safety of the principals was at stake. Their names must never be known, yet this case proved once and for all that Shirley Harrison had become one of the most sensitive psychics in the history of modern parapsychology.

This case involved a kidnapping. The story developed circumstances weird enough to entrance the most jaded kidnap-fiction fan. At the conclusion of this case Shirley herself admitted that her power of ESP proved greater than she had ever allowed herself to imagine it to be.

This story is true. The facts have been verified and are accurate, attested to by the mother of the young kidnap victim. But her continuing fear, real or imagined, from the kidnapper has required that we change the names to insure her continued safety and anonymity. This we promised to do, and have done.

On a May morning in 1964, Shirley was telephoned by the pastor of one of the most prominent parishes in New England. (Although Shirley's telephone had been unlisted for more than two years to avoid the deluge of calls she had been receiving.) Shirley remembers the initial call in the case clearly. The pastor asked her to find a child. This was not unusual. She had been asked countless times to find not only the neighborhood children late from school, but also their stray pets.

However, this was to be no lighthearted, local, guessing game. As the pastor explained his request, Shirley had to remind herself to remain calm and uninvolved emotionally. What she called an inner quietude was necessary in order to practice her subtle craft. It required her utter serenity.

She assured the pastor of her complete co-operation. Yes, she would try to help. Yet he must understand that she could not promise results of any kind, she told the minister. She could, however, offer the comfort and serenity of her living room, in order, perhaps, that her psychic powers should be at their best. There was no mention of money, nor did Shirley expect any. It was her custom to help people in distress without any financial consideration.

The pastor arrived at Shirley's house in the Salmon Falls area of Buxton, Maine, the next morning. With him, that day, was a woman.

Shirley's impression of her is that she was under great stress, struggling hard to control herself. She appeared to be of Shirley's own age. She was of Scandinavian fairness of complexion, and her hair was blonde, yet her eyes were ringed with dark hollows and her face was pallid. Her manner was nervous and she relied on the pastor's arm to climb the steps onto Shirley's porch. She carried a jacket of a size to fit a pre-school child.

Without introductions — which in any case must be ommitted here at the mother's request — she said to Shirley, "I've got to have something to hold on to or I will lose my mind."

"On that first visit," remembers Shirley, "she had only one question: 'Is my little one going to die?'"

"Can you tell me?" the mother pleaded.

"I don't know," said Shirley with all the kindness of the discreet truth, "but I am going to try to help him."

Shirley ushered the pastor and his parishioner into her

house. She offered them hot tea and rolls which they accepted gratefully.

Recalling that first visit years later, Shirley said that although she prefers to know as little as possible about a person she is seeking via clairvoyance — such knowledge can only lead her to misinterpret what she is to learn — the woman told her story in detail.

The lady was the divorced mother of a little boy. The ex-husband, she said, had been in trouble with the police for many years. In fact, their marriage had broken up when the wife learned of her husband's prison record. Prior to their separating, they had adopted a little boy. Now the wife feared for the safety of their child and for her own safety as well. She explained to Shirley that when the divorce was granted, her ex-husband had threatened revenge, a threat he seemed to have carried out with passionate perversity.

It was on a morning several months after their divorce, for which the negotiations proved even more stormy than the marriage, that the ex-husband called again. This time he had pleaded for a visit with the little boy. After all, he had implored, he loved him also. The mother was deeply moved. She saw this was more than a mere harrassing call. She overruled her initial impulse to cut off the conversation with a final no. In fact, she agreed. He may come for a short visit with the child. When he arrived at her house, she went for a walk, leaving her ex-husband and the boy alone in the house. She planned to return in a few hours.

When she returned, her worst foreboding proved true. She discovered the house locked from the outside. She rushed into the garage where she found her car tires slashed. Her telephone line had been cut. Worst of all, her son was missing.

This was evidence of her ex-husband's cunning. Such a man, she knew and feared, could harm her child. She ran to a neighbor's house and called the police.

The police took a report from an hysterical woman. They acted with characteristic and reasonable coolness. They waited. From dozens of similar complaints, domestic quarrels seem to dominate a police officer's duties; they knew from experience that the child often is returned within a few hours, a few days at most. After all, out of several thousand such cases, only one proves statistically to be an actual kidnapping.

A week passed with no report of her son. Although the police may, indeed, have been searching, they had no positive report to make to the mother. The mother fell ill from anxiety and from lack of sleep. She called her pastor. The pastor called Shirley.

In the mother's mind her divorced husband was capable of committing still another crime, perhaps a crime of violence. Her son could be an innocent victim, a victim not only of a crime but also a hostage to save the father's freedom and perhaps his life during his commission of future crimes.

The mother handed Shirley the little boy's jacket. She also handed her a photograph of the child. Despite her best efforts to remain calmly objective, Shirley was deeply moved.

"He was as beautiful to me," said Shirley, "as if he were my own child."

In fact, Shirley's twins were of the same age as that child. On that particular morning, her twins were at a neighbor's house, nearby, playing happily and safely. This woman's son, Shirley realized, was not happy or safe. Shirley felt a deep kinship to the troubled, frightened, woman.

"I concentrated like anyone would do to solve a problem," said Shirley recalling that morning of their first visit. "I asked myself, 'Is he alive?' If I got a strong, positive, feeling, I would know that he was alive. This is the intuitive part of ESP. There is no deductive reasoning involved at this point because there is no real point of reference.

"I had learned to wait for impressions to come to me," said Shirley. "There are long moments of nothing. Then, suddenly, a set of facts will spring into my mind. It is almost as if someone had told them to me. I write them down.

"Then I reflect on the facts," she continued. "It seems as though my mind feeds these facts into some kind of mental computer. Then my mind weighs that evidence. If I get a strong feeling that the conclusions and the facts are right, I write them down again. If not, then I discard the thoughts and keep concentrating. I keep on waiting for facts that feel, intuitively, correct, that feel right."

Shirley held the little boy's jacket and the photograph of him. The pastor and the mother waited anxiously, hanging on Shirley's expression of calm expectation. They concentrated on Shirley's face as if it were the seismograph of her inner awareness.

Shirley began to write with a short blunt pencil on a blank page of a notebook. Once again, she summoned her powers to achieve an inner peace. She wanted no preoccupations to interfere with what she hoped to achieve. Once again, like a musician composing a score, her hand moved furiously on the notebook. She wrote words, key words, words to guide her as the remainder of their associated meaning was forming in her mind.

After what may have been five minutes of intense silence, Shirley looked up into the mother's anguished eyes.

"He is all right," said Shirley. "You are going to get him back. . ."

The question "when?" was urgently asked by all in the room, although it was not spoken aloud.

". . . By the end of the summer," said Shirley.

"Those were the thoughts which I felt, and knew intuitively were correct," Shirley recalls, thinking back to that meeting.

Later, discussing that critical moment in the case with me, Shirley admitted that if she had learned the child was dead, she would have hesitated to tell the mother.

"I would have taken the minister aside," she said. "I would have told him I had learned bad information. I would have reminded him of the wide margin of error in ESP. I would have said that I am not sure — but it looks bad."

I knew that in the Olenchuk case, in some ways similar to this one, Shirley had said just that; that it looked bad, that she felt the Olenchuk girl was dead. However, in this case, she had a positive feeling. More than that, she had said when the child would be returned.

Shirley told her visitors she had given them all the information she could learn in one day. She invited them to come back in a few days. She assured them the safety and whereabouts of the little boy would remain uppermost in her mind.

A week later, her visitors were seated once more in her living room. Shirley noticed the mother looked rested and relieved. Only her confidence in Shirley's integrity could have granted her this composure.

Once again, Shirley placed the notebook on her lap. She took the blunt pencil in her right hand. She began to write a few words, and after a short interval she read from her page as if from a psychic shorthand.

"He has sold the car," said Shirley quietly. "He has sold it to a Black man down South. They are continuing by bus toward the Mexican border."

And then Shirley proved once again that she was uncannily accurate in another phase of parapsychology, that is in the psychic diagnosis of medical problems. This time, she diagnosed by clairvoyance across at least a thousand miles. She told the mother that the little boy "has an earache."

"He has been taken to the outpatient clinic of a hospital in a large southwestern city. He has an earache and a sore throat," she repeated.

As was to become a necessary requirement to her ESP in many cases, Shirley asked her visitors to return in a few days. In this case I was to learn that there were at least a dozen psychic visits between the mother and Shirley (alone, since the mother no longer needed the company of her pastor after the initial meetings). "We had become friends," said Shirley, "and we've been friends ever since."

At the next meeting, Shirley greeted the mother warmly. This time she introduced her to her own twins, Michael and Eric. The two little boys played quietly in the living room while Shirley opened the notebook and prepared herself as usual to learn what she could about the visitor's son.

This time, Shirley reported, "the little boy is at the racetrack watching cars." Once again, she reported on his medical status: "He has been given shots for travel to Mexico," she said.

It was during this session, with Michael and Eric playing on the floor between them, that the mother asked Shirley whether her son were wearing "his special orthopedic shoes?"

"No," said Shirley without any hesitation and without any writing on the notebook.

"He is wearing a pair of little red sneakers. And," she added, "he is carrying a little red suitcase."

And then Shirley told the mother a fact which was to prove a controversial factor in the case.

"He is in a cloistered place," said Shirley. "He is in the care of nuns."

The mother knew that her ex-husband, the father and technical kidnapper of their little boy, was a devout Roman Catholic. Despite his criminal record and many years in prison to which he had been returned again and again, he often sought the counsel of a priest. One priest, in particular, had been especially close to him. That priest, she knew, had been transferred down South. She knew the city and the church because her ex-husband had mentioned them several times. She telephoned the priest.

Had her ex-husband been to see him? Was their son with him?

The priest denied that her ex-husband had been to see him.

As Shirley recalls, when this report reached her, she secretly doubted the priest's word. It just did not seem right to her. She knew, however, that time would tell.

Oddly enough, this report, although negative, reaffirmed, rather than caused Shirley to doubt that she was, in fact, getting psychic information about the right person. She felt she was right on target, and she looked forward with rapt curiosity to future feats of clairvoyance.

During the mother's next visit to Salmon Falls and to Shirley's peaceful living room, Shirley pinpointed the kidnapper with complete accuracy. Speaking with astonishing self-confidence in clear everyday English, with no hint of Puritan euphemisms so often encountered in psychic so-called readings, Shirley astonished not only the attentive mother but herself as well.

Shirley named the kidnapper's hotel. She actually described it. She said the hotel name on the marquee had a letter missing and she told which one. She described neighboring buildings, especially the shop fronts and business signs on both sides of the street. She actually named the partners of a law firm whose names were cast in bronze on a massive dark oak door. She said there was a "Waitress wanted" sign in a steamy window. She said there was a cheap bar across the street from the hotel. She named the street signs at the intersection. She said there was a fire station nearby. And, she named the city.

The mother, who had been taking notes rapidly, picked up the telephone. She called information in the city Shirley named only seconds before. She asked for the hotel Shirley named. To her astonishment, and to Shirley's satisfaction, she dialed the number and spoke to the desk clerk. She asked for the kidnapper by name, her ex-husband.

The desk clerk gave her the number of his room, and while the mother was on the line, he rang the room.

There was no answer.

"I don't think he's back from work yet," said the clerk, and then he added quickly, "Wait a minute. Here he is. I see him coming into the lobby!"

The mother could actually hear the clerk paging the kidnapper to the phone.

"I broke the connection," said the mother in her detailed account of this story. "I called the FBI." She also called her pastor. The pastor had a colleague in that city. He called him immediately. He asked him to go to that hotel, to ask for the kidnapper and for the child. He also asked his friend to casually survey the neighborhood of the hotel and he relayed Shirley's information learned via clairvoyance and recorded in notes.

When the colleague called back, he said it was as if Shirley had been looking at a photograph of the neighborhood. Her names and descriptions were accurate in detail. However, he reported, the person had left the hotel. There had been a child with him, a little boy.

This time Shirley's clairvoyance was fully corroborated, fully affirmed, not only by the desk clerk in candid conversation from the hotel, but also by the minister's incredulous description of the neighborhood. The minister had, in fact, confirmed the "Waitress wanted" sign, the law firm with names in bronze, a fire station diagonally across the street from the hotel. He confirmed that the hotel did, indeed, have a letter missing in its sign on the marquee. Not only that, he confirmed that Shirley had correctly named the streets at the intersection.

Shirley had described the area with photographic realism, and she was jubilant.

"It's as though I were right there!" she exulted.

"We were so excited," she remembers. "We were actually tracking down, actually pinpointing the kidnapper in his hotel."

Not only that, Shirley felt she was learning to develop detailed and accurate information about one person in particular, a pre-selected person, as he moved at random across country.

This, she knew, was a breakthrough in the art of parapsychology.

This was information retrieval, indeed! It was an extrasensory feat far surpassing the expertise of even the most sophisticated, state-of-the-art, communication relay systems, systems actually in place on satellites then in orbit around the planet.

To Shirley, dedicated as she was to research in the subtle craft, this was also a personal triumph.

"It was one of the most stunning moments in my life!" she exulted.

Yet, Shirley was to learn still more about this case.

A few days later, the pastor, the mother, and Shirley met again in Shirley's living room. These meetings by now had become regular events in the routine of their lives.

This time Shirley was eager to welcome the new knowledge. Her anticipation was high. This was a good sign to her. Depression, anger, resentment, any negative feeling at all, tended to smother Shirley's powers. She needed a positive frame of mind to give her confidence in her craft.

Seated in the cool living room that summer day, Shirley spoke calmly with carefully elocuted phrases. I was to learn that sometimes in similar situations she spoke as if she were teaching children to spell difficult words.

She dictated the license number of a car. She gave another, longer, number. She named a used car dealer, a Ford dealer. She named a city, Culver City, California. She described a car by make and color. She said the kidnapper had bought that car.

The missing boy's mother telephoned a private detective in Colorado who was a personal friend of her family. She asked him if he would please use this information to find out if her ex-husband had bought such a car from the dealer Shirley Harrison described in Culver City, California.

The private detective agreed to assign one of his investigators to that case. They checked all the used car dealers in that city and discovered the record of the sale of that type car to a man with the name of the ex-husband. The detective's report of the car sale and the buyer's name was given to the police who checked into the matter further.

They verified that a man by that name had, indeed, bought a car of that description in that city and from that specific dealer. But *they said* it was not the same person. It was another person with the same name!

Shirley was astounded and deeply puzzled by this revelation. She had found a man who had bought a car in California where she had "seen" that event take place. But, it seemed to her distress, to be the wrong person, despite the fact that he had the same name.

To this day, Shirley and the mother still wonder about this situation. Was it really a different man who coincidentally had the same name? Or was it really the ex-husband, but that fact denied by the police for some hidden reason?

The fact remained that in that case this was another breakthrough in Shirley's search to understand ESP. This time, oddly enough, she had scientific support, support to corroborate what she had just learned.

Only months previously, William G. Roll of the Psychical Research Foundation in Durham, North Carolina, had conducted a careful experiment with Shirley. Afterwards, he described his procedures and his conclusions in a carefully detailed print-out. This was one of the methods by which scientists in the field of parapsychology kept each other abreast of their latest discoveries.

Roll wrote Shirley that not only had she been able to select cards and numbers far more accurately than chance alone would select them, but that she had also selected them according to their previous handlers. Shirley recognized some similarity between Roll's conclusion and her feat of ESP that day if the police record was accurate.

During the weeks that followed, the mother and her pastor, at Shirley's fervent urging, continued to follow up in their own psychic search into the truth in the real world of Shirley's clairvoyance.

Subsequently, the pastor was to learn that Shirley had been right once more. He was able to gain a reluctant admission from the priest the mother had earlier telephoned. The priest explained that he was not permitted to give out information about those who came to him for help. But, he did admit that a man and a boy visited him at the time a lady had called inquiring about them. The priest had counseled the man and had arranged for the little boy to live with nuns for several weeks while the man found work.

The mother eventually learned from certificates of vaccination in her son's red suitcase, a new red, plaid, one, that he had, in fact, been given shots. She learned also that her little boy had seen "cars on a racing track" and that he had watched fire engines from a hotel window.

Shirley's clairvoyance was proving accurate in instance after instance.

Despite the fact that police had located, with help of private detectives, a man who bought a car in California and who had the same name as the mother's ex-husband, Shirley was never able to learn if her ESP had been accurate.

Yet, when the boy was found, the authorities reported that the mother's ex-husband had indeed sold his original car and was driving another, a used car bought in the West. There is no logical explanation for this discrepancy between what Shirley saw in the car lot in California and the actual purchase of a used car in a western state. The astonishing fact remains, that the kidnapper did buy a used car and was found driving it. Unfortunately, the authorities, while contacting the mother and telling her that her son was alive and well, did not provide any description of that car or where it had been purchased.

Neither were they able to elicit from the FBI any confirmation of the role of Shirley's ESP in the capture of the kidnapper. The FBI answered our query for information by saying they treated information from psychics just as they would treat, and act on, any other information. No more, no less.

The heart of the matter, put simply, is that Shirley proved once again in this case that she was able to pinpoint and describe the location of things she had thought about.

Try as she would to understand her amazing and precise powers, only a few factors seem clear.

One factor is that Shirley in this case of a cross-country kidnapping, over a three-month interim, sought six or eight delays, delays of a few days to a week between visits to her living room. She seemed to require a period of incubation. As Shirley confirmed, these were periods in which she did not in any way concentrate on the problem of the kidnapped little boy. In fact, it was as though the problem had to be forgotten in order to be solved.

And then, at the appointed time, sometimes in the company of her own twin boys, sometimes in the company of the mother and the pastor, and sometimes with all assembled in her living room, Shirley directed her psychic energy in an intense and incredible concentration.

Simultaneously, as if to keep up with her racing mind, she

scribbled words in a psychic shorthand on a page in a note-book on her lap. She wrote key words to record the psychic illuminations she received.

Shirley herself does not know what actually happened in these seconds and minutes of intense concentration during which she learned much that we have found to be accurate.

Neither, perhaps, may we know. But, as all investigators must, I continued pursuing the facts of other cases in which Shirley Harrison was involved. And, equally important, I returned again and again to interview Shirley in depth about her feelings during these episodes in her life. Only in that way could I focus on and define what it is that she does and perhaps learn more about her powers and how they work.

Vanished Wife

Shirley Harrison's ability to focus on and solve the apparently impossible tasks of locating missing persons, from a little boy abducted in a cross-country kidnapping to a victim of a murder in an old abandoned barn, was no longer some imagined flight of fancy, or the claim of a psychic seeking notoriety. By painstaking checking with authorities involved in these cases, it has been possible to thoroughly document Shirley's uncommon success.

Another case, the story of a vanished wife who simply disappeared after an argument with her pharmacist husband, provided another clear opportunity to investigate Shirley's remarkable clairvoyance.

Once again, it was my job to confirm and corroborate the stories I had heard about Shirley Harrison's psychic life. I needed official proof that events of which she was said to have had paranormal knowledge had, indeed, occurred.

I first interviewed Shirley in depth, asking her to search back through her memories of that particular case. I transcribed her recollections and sent them back to her for reaffirmation. And then, as a dyed-in-the-wool cynic and dedicated doubter, I required continual confirmation from sources other than Shirley herself, reliable and fascinating as she proved to be. I contacted both the husband of the missing woman and others intimately involved in the search. I checked medical, police and press records made at the time.

My search led me to the dispatcher at the Old Orchard Police Department. She recognized the events as I described them based on information I had learned from Shirley. She referred me to Deputy Chief Paul Tibbetts, who, she said, had been assigned to the case.

Tibbetts searched his memory of "some time ago," and then

as is not unusual with a professional police officer, he remembered the case clearly. He asked me to hold the phone while he pulled the report from his files.

"Jean Lacroix was Acting Chief at the time," said Tibbetts. And the State Police Homicide man on the case was Detective Paul Hooper.

"The first report came from Bob St. Laurent," said Tibbetts. "He's the pharmacist here in town."

Tibbetts told me he had set in motion the usual administrative search procedure. He sent out a missing person teletype . He questioned the missing woman's parents who lived nearby. Together with Detective Hooper, he inspected the area around the family home. Many people in the neighborhood helped look for her.

"Where could she have gone?" Tibbetts remembers wondering. "Had she changed her name? Had she run off with another guy?" There was no indication she had done so. "Was she emotionally or mentally disturbed?"

Days passed, days of cold, dull, bitter weather. "We couldn't find the woman or any trace of her," Tibbetts explained.

Shirley Harrison's memory of ten years back to that night when Bob St. Laurent first called remains an emotional one.

"He begged for help," said Shirley. "I was filled with foreboding.

"I became deeply upset from the first sound of his voice on the phone," she remembers. "He was a stranger to me. His voice was that of a man in an emotionally overwrought state. He said his wife had left the house and had not returned. He somehow expected me to find her.

"I felt an overpowering, depressing dread," said Shirley. "I told him outright that I did not want to be asked to help him. I used every excuse. I said I was busy cleaning house, that family matters required every second of my time. Finally, I told him frankly and truly that I was not feeling well.

"The fact is," said Shirley, "that my feelings were not related to my own health. Because by then I had begun to concentrate on his wife. And I dreaded what I knew I would have to tell him."

When I interviewed Bob St. Laurent, he seemed anxious to relate everything in his memory of the events during those weeks after his wife disappeared.

His story was an eerie one. St. Laurent said that he was in his front yard raking leaves on a snowless, frozen lawn, when he was approached by a woman he knew to be Alice Castro.

Alice Castro was an elderly lady who had lived in Old Orchard Beach. St. Laurent said that Alice did not speak to him at first. Instead, she looked directly into his eyes and handed him a note. St. Laurent said he opened the note and found a telephone number.

Alice Castro then said to him, "Why don't you call this woman? She will help you find your wife!"

"I said, 'thank you,'" St. Laurent recalls, "and I put the note in my pocket. As Alice Castro reached the corner of my street, she turned back and seemed to say to me, 'Call her. She will know.' And she turned the corner and disappeared."

By this time, St. Laurent was desperate. He had lost his wife. There was no word from police, from family or from friends where she might be. He loved her and he wanted her back.

"I acted out of desperation," said St. Laurent. "I went into the house and called the number in Alice Castro's note."

"He called me again and again," said Shirley, recalling the hours and days that followed that first call.

"I have been in surgery and I have not fully recovered," Shirley recalls telling St. Laurent at the time. He persisted.

Finally, Shirley gave in. "You know that I cannot promise you anything with ESP," she said to him. "I cannot promise to be helpful to you or to her, not in any way."

He assured Shirley that he understood.

"I can offer compassion," said Shirley, "and I will use all my strength to learn what there is for me to know about her. I will try," Shirley told him.

"Although he continued to call me with single-minded persistence," said Shirley, recalling the days and hours that followed, "again I had to tell him that I could learn nothing. The truth is that I felt such foreboding I could not bring myself to look at the facts. He called what seemed to me to be continually, yet I could learn nothing specific. No words triggered complete thoughts in my mind. I felt only dread.

"And then after a week," she said, "a week of trying to evade his questions, I felt resigned to the fact now apparent to me that I was going to do it. For the first time in a week I was able to relax with the conviction that I could help find her.

"Quietly, reflectively," said Shirley, "I made an estimate of myself, an estimate of my health, of my powers of clairvoyance which might then have been ebbing. I recognized this fact with objectivity."

At this point in Shirley's memory of the matter, Bob St. Laurent telephoned once again. The police had found nothing, he said. "It is hopeless."

Shirley's response, she recalls, was a spontaneous and clearly detailed, clairvoyant account of his domestic life and problem. She told St. Laurent that his wife had suffered a depression rooted in her feelings about her childhood. She said that her emotional conflict triggered an irreversible although carefully concealed depression in the young woman. She said that the young woman was a trained laboratory technician, and that she would be found in a place called, and here for the first time she was uncertain, but it sounded to her like "Lawrence."

The husband called the police in Lawrence, Mass., 100 miles west. There was no record of his wife known to them in that town.

He called Shirley back and said that her knowledge of their domestic life, about recent problems, had been accurate. Yes, they had quarreled. There had, indeed, been a traumatic episode in their life. Yes, she was indeed a laboratory technician.

He said he had not told the police of these quarrels because he was ashamed of his role in them. He asked Shirley if she could tell him anything more about his wife which could help him find her.

This time Shirley read to him what she had written in clear open letters on a pad beside the telephone after their last conversation a few minutes earlier.

"I began to get a lot more facts," said Shirley, "facts about family things that were going on. I began to get facts about things that had troubled the missing woman.

"I reported this information to him. 'Is this so?' I asked."

"'Yes, this is true,' he said. 'What you're picking up is true.'

"I said, 'All right, this is where I feel she is. She is behind a wall, a walled in area. She is on Route 5. I keep getting the name St. Laurent, St. Laurent, St. Laurent, over and over and over. I now feel that what I had interpreted to be Lawrence was, in fact, St. Laurent. She is behind a wall near a trailer on Route 5. I see a green house with white doors.'

"He said, 'Well I live on Route 5.' "

"So you do.

" 'That's all?' he asked.

" 'That's all,' I said. 'But, one more thing. I get no sense of direction in regard to her whereabouts.'

"That's all I could get that day.

"He called me back the next morning," Shirley remembered. "He said he had been out all night driving up and down Route 5. He had been to see a friend who had a house trailer and he had looked exhaustively all around the trailer. He said he had searched along both sides of all the walls on Route 5 that he had seen during his drive.

"Keep looking," I said. "I still felt empowered by the information I had written on my pad.

"Keep looking," I repeated. "Behind the wall, the wall. Beside the trailer. I get your name and then I repeated it again, St. Laurent, St. Laurent. And on Route 5. Over and over.

"That was all I could tell him. I couldn't seem to learn any more."

Bob St. Laurent's own account of the events that followed this phone call in which Shirley reaffirmed her psychic information provides a detailed focus on those events.

"Three weeks after my wife disappeared," he said, "I was still anxious and bewildered by Shirley's clairvoyant information about my wife and her family. It just happened to be my mother-in-law's birthday. I was in an agony of dread and apprehension. They stopped in to visit. I had preoccupied myself with fixing up the house against the day of my wife's return. I hoped she would walk once again into my life," he said.

He explained that the mother and father-in-law sat in the kitchen which he had newly remodeled. He remembered his father-in-law saying: "It is your birthday and she has never forgotten you on this day. If you are going to hear from her, it will be today."

"We had coffee," St. Laurent remembers, "and then they went home.

"I was left in the kitchen alone, with my mother who had come to take care of the children."

In despair, he remembers, he put his head down on the table and pondered what Shirley had told him.

"What am I going to do?" he asked himself.

It was then that he heard water leaking in the bathroom. He went in and saw water dripping down through the new ceiling tiles. He got a chair and a flashlight, climbed up and removed several tiles. He flashed his light in under the roof.

"I could see where water was coming in and decided to go look outside," he said. "It had been very cold for three weeks and that day, for the first time, it was warm. It was so warm that the snow was melting in the streets of Old Orchard and sluicing down the gutters into the ocean. The snow on my roof was melting, too, and the water was backing up into my bathroom.

"I went outside," he said, "to see if I could locate the leak.

"I had a trailer parked in the yard beside the wall under my porch. It was not the kind of trailer you live in. It was the kind of trailer you hitch to your car and take to the dump. I waded around it in the slush. I knocked some ice and snow off my roof and then started back into my house.

"I flashed the light so I could return in the same tracks I came out in."

It was at that moment that St. Laurent saw her.

"My flashlight flickered, if only for an instant, onto the sole and then onto a foot," he said.

"I recognized it instantly. It was my wife. I had found her. She was under the house lying behind the wall I had built that summer to enclose the front porch."

He does not remember how long it was before he returned to the kitchen. But it was then, he said, that he called Shirley Harrison.

"I told her I had found my wife. I told her she was there behind the wall on Route 5. I told her that I had parked a trailer beside the wall and I told her what kind of trailer it was."

"I know," said Shirley.

"Call the police."

The police report from Deputy Chief Paul Tibbetts appears to confirm the details of the husband's account of how he found his wife.

"It was cold miserable weather," said Tibbetts of that time ten years earlier. "We had ten days of below zero — 20 below zero — and then a thaw, what we call a January thaw. There was ice and snow leaking into everybody's roofs all over the area.

"When I got to St. Laurent's residence, he led me around the house and under it through a hole in the wall, and there she was. . ."

I asked Tibbetts whether he knew Alice Castro, the old woman who put Bob St. Laurent in touch so mysteriously with Shirley Harrison?

"Sure," he said. "She used to live on Staples Street right in back of the pharmacy. She's not there any more," he said. "I don't know where she is."

Again in this puzzling case of Robert St. Laurent, it had been possible to trace what Shirley Harrison had said and done back to those people intimately involved in the case.

The husband, Robert St. Laurent, had confirmed the details of what Shirley had told him, and verified that he had finally found his wife's body in a place that had been so graphically described by Shirley Harrison.

There was no mistaking the facts as he described them from his memory of those trying days. There was no mistaking the fact that Shirley Harrison had proved accurate in what she had forseen. But again, the "how?" of what she had done eluded explanation.

Some of that "how?", the explanation of her own minutes, hours, and days of psychic efforts, I realized must come from detailed talks with Shirley herself and probing questions to seek illumination on the way she achieved these uncanny insights from her mind that proved so graphically real in fact.

With these documented cases verified by all participants, it would be necessary to retrace the life of Shirley Harrison from her youth through every significant event. That biography, I hoped, would reveal some secrets of her powers.

Newsboy Murder

By this time in my search for documentation of the psychic powers of Shirley Harrison, I had learned that Shirley's powers of clairvoyance involved her in traumatic and desperate events in the personal lives of many people. I learned that Shirley helped if she were asked, even if it was difficult for her to do so. Apparently, hers was a responsibility thrust upon her, an obligation inseparable from her powers.

The tragic case of a missing newsboy once again focussed my attention on her uncanny abilities to perceive facts; facts that public officials sometimes refused to acknowledge or believe. This case in some ways proved even more remarkable as I uncovered more nuances in the psychic phenomenon of Shirley Harrison.

The case I explored and documented for this chapter of Psychic Search involves a missing newsboy, Cyrus Everett. I had learned that according to eye witnesses, Shirley pinpointed the location of his body with absolute accuracy hundreds of miles away. I saw letters written at the time, acknowledged by their authors, confirming that Shirley had once again done the impossible.

One of the witnesses critical to verification of this case is Linnwood Ross. He was Deputy Secretary of State of Maine at the time.

Other witnesses include two State Police detectives who also attested to Shirley's role in this case. They are Otis LaBree and Camille Carrier. Both worked on the missing newsboy case at the time.

The case was controversial. In fact, Shirley's uncanny clairvoyance in the matter of the location of the body of Cyrus Everett was disputed and disputed passionately. It still is by some.

The editor and publisher of the home town newspaper the
boy was delivering on his last, fateful errand, denied that
Shirley had described the location of his body. When I cited
the official evidence from police records, from first-hand affidavits, from eye witnesses to the contrary, he remained un-
believing.

"She was wrong," he said. "Totally wrong. It is a myth."

I probed further. I asked if the body was found on the
Cheney place as Shirley clairvoyantly predicted and as police
confirmed.

"No, it was not," he replied.

But I learned that the people of Fort Fairfield, Maine, popu-
lation 6,000, actually countermanded the authority of their
sheriff and deputies when they refused to concede that what
Shirley had predicted was true. The Fort Fairfield town coun-
cil requested outside police officials to investigate the crime
Shirley described, a crime their town officers denied had ever
been committed.

Strong feelings were acted out as if on a stage in that remote town in which this tragedy occurred. The story revealed
itself in police reports, press clippings and interviews.

I learned that Shirley pinpointed not only the location of
the body of Cyrus Everett; she also described the manner of
his murder and those people who were to become prime sus-
pects in the crime.

I learned that Shirley described them in a way that police
termed "accurate in every detail."

In fact, the case is still open. The murderer of Cyrus
Everett has not been convicted for the crime. Whether or
not another murder, this time of a waitress, Mrs. Donna
Mauch, 26, who was bludgeoned to death in Fort Fairfield
mere months after the murder of Cyrus Everett, is related
to the Cyrus Everett murder, is not known.

What remains to be investigated dating back to the Cyrus
Everett case is the fact that a suspect who lives in that area
is presently serving a long sentence in Connecticut. He was
convicted of a similar murder there after the Everett episode
took place.

This case in its perplexing ramifications has been reconstructed here from press and police reports, from personal
interviews, and from Shirley's notes and memory. At the
time, of course, the participants in this true drama could not

have known what was yet to happen. Shirley herself was not to know until months later that her perceptions were so dramatically accurate.

On December 26th, 1964, in Fort Fairfield, Maine, a small town on the New Brunswick border of Canada in the extreme northern part of the state, Cyrus Everett, 14, set out to collect for his paper route. The boy never returned.

His mother, Mrs. Mary Everett, a housekeeper well known and trusted in the town, said she "knew that night" that her son was dead. Her conviction was in the form of foreboding, a symptom of anxiety familiar to all mothers.

Cyrus was her only child. Mary Everett was divorced. Her son's paper route was important to their livelihood.

The boy was small for his age but nervy, neighbors remember, and determined to succeed even against odds; odds not in his favor that night. The weather was freezing rain, turning to snow. Nevertheless, he had hopes, his mother remembers; hopes of collecting Christmas bonuses from his customers. She buttoned his heavy coat.

The boy carried a collection pouch and a route book listing all who owed him money, up to $50. That was a lot of money to the boy and his mother. When Cyrus did not come home that evening, Mary Everett called the Fort Fairfield sheriff's office.

Yes, they knew Cyrus. They would look for him. Mary Everett described his paper route.

But the sheriff did not find Cyrus. In despair, Mary Everett actually prayed that her son had struck out for a few days of freedom on his own. Perhaps he had sought work at a nearby farm where there was always work to be done. But there was no phone call that night to Mary Everett from a neighboring mother to say Cyrus was warm and fed and helping with the farm chores. That Christmas holiday was one of unforgetable tragedy for Mary Everett.

The mysterious disappearance of the 14-year-old boy was reported in the press including the widely circulated Bangor Daily News. At least one other concerned mother began to worry about Cyrus; Christine Donham of Island Falls, Maine, the mother of Shirley Harrison.

Christine Donham had been a schoolteacher for many years. She knew that children in that rural area did not often run away from home. She felt somehow personally responsible.

She wrote to her daughter and asked, "What do you think has happened to that little Fort Fairfield boy?"

Shirley received her mother's letter and read it with compassion. She resolved to test her ESP, to save this child if she could.

That particular morning she was planning to go shopping with her friend and mentor in matters parapsychological, Mrs. Ruth Hyde. When Ruth Hyde drove into Shirley's yard, Shirley stuffed her mother's letter into her handbag and went out to join her friend.

By coincidence, Shirley recalls, her friend mentioned casually the mystery of the whereabouts of "the little Fort Fairfield boy."

Shirley's answer seemed spontaneous to Ruth Hyde. Shirley said that "he is under water . . . lying under a log . . . a log so heavy it will have to be moved by a bulldozer or by dynamite . . . he is on the Cheney place. . ." said Shirley. ". . . near Fort Fairfield . . . he was murdered, struck on the back of the head . . . his money is gone."

Ruth Hyde made a note of Shirley's astonishing psychic utterings. She wrote them down on the first scrap of paper she could find in her handbag. It was the back of a light bill.

The important point in my mind years later is that she made her notes promptly and without interpreting them and that she kept the scrap of paper, that all-important light bill, where she could find it. It seemed to her that by so doing it might serve as a pathway to an explanation of ESP.

Shirley's own memory of what happened during those seconds in which she pinpointed the body of the boy is disarmingly simple.

"I was just told," she said. "I overheard it. It's like eavesdropping." After a few seconds recollection she added, "I said it before I thought it. The truth is," Shirley concluded, "I don't know where that information came from."

Neither did she know if the information was accurate.

Later in that week, Shirley Harrison was introduced as a guest speaker for a local convention being held at the Holiday Inn located at Exit 8 off the Maine Turnpike in Westbrook, Maine.

Shirley was lauded that night as a pioneering scientist inquiring into the source of her uncanny knowledge. Shirley spoke of the origins of ESP in her childhood, of the questions it compelled her to ponder. Shirley revealed herself to be a person with special knowledge who cannot stand by and wait for somebody else to find the answer to her questions.

Shirley told her audience she had evidence that her ESP could predict real events. There have been examples of fore-knowledge, she said. There are many such cases in the Bible. "I have many examples from my own life, examples I have shared with you."

Referring to carefully kept notes of her lecture, Shirley recalled she had told her audience that the really complex and unfamiliar part of the mind is still virtually unexplored, except by a tiny handful of scientists. Shirley assured her audience that ESP is a natural occurrence and she chided some rational intellectuals for not admitting ESP existed.

"ESP has been measured," she said. "It is part of the scientific concepts of such great thinkers as Einstein and Freud." In fact, she said that an understanding of ESP, or at least a curiosity about it, is indispensable to any inquiry into the nature of thought itself.

Incredibly, uncannily, said Shirley, she had sometimes known of events that had not yet happened, events in the real world. She had, on occasion, achieved clairvoyance.

At the close of her lecture that day, Shirley was to experience once again what she had long since come to expect. The conventioners might pay lip service to scientific goals requiring years of careful research, but they really wanted to see ESP perform miracles right there and then.

"That way," they told her, "we can actually experience what you are describing."

"Fair enough," said Shirley. She would try. She could not promise anything.

The first question came from the audience. "Where is that newspaper boy?"

Shirley said that she had been asked that question not only by her mother in the mail earlier that week, but also by her friend and now, once again, by a person in this audience.

"What about Cyrus Everett?" the questioner from the audience asked again.

Theorists exploring the mystery of ESP rarely have to prove their theories on the spot before an audience. Here and now the burden of proof was on Shirley. If she were proved wrong that day, everything she had said of what she believed in would be discredited.

Shirley repeated to the conventioners out there in the dark in front of her podium what she had said to Ruth Hyde. She told them the boy was on the Cheney place, that he was in water, that he was under a log or something very heavy because she had the almost suffocating feeling of weight; so much weight that it would have to be removed with a bulldozer or by dynamite. She said he had been hit too hard on the head and that his money was gone.

At that answer, which must have startled at least a few of the conventioners, a gentleman rose to his feet.

He offered to telephone a friend in Fort Fairfield and inquire if he knew of a Cheney place.

"I wish you would," said Shirley.

In the minds of some conventioners, her information may have been learned through inside means and not reported in the press. They suspected that because Shirley had been born in "the county," as Aroostook County is known throughout Maine, probably she had relatives in Fort Fairfield.

Whatever the motives of the questioner, or the feelings of others in her audience, what transpired next set in motion a chain reaction of psychic intrigue which has not been solved to this day.

The man from the audience returned from the telephone. He announced that his friend in Fort Fairfield had confirmed that there was, indeed, a Cheney place. It was called Cheney's Grove.

Shirley's impression of the reaction of the audience to this confirmation is that believers believed and skeptics doubted. Some seemed stunned.

She knew that if part of her clairvoyant information was correct, the rest often fit into place like pieces of a puzzle. She suggested to any residents of that area that they begin a search or institute one. If the pieces fit, then Cyrus Everett was dead. He had been murdered and possibly robbed. I knew Shirley often pursued her own investigation into the accuracy of her ESP. Shirley's follow-up was to prove unusually intriguing in this case, as was mine. Further complications awaited both of us.

I subsequently learned that the man in Fort Fairfield who confirmed the existence of the Cheney Grove was Kingdon

Harvey, owner and editor of the Fort Fairfield Review and past president of the Maine Press Association.

"Sure, I remember," said Kingdon years later.

"Of course it was murder. I knew that. Everybody knew that. In fact, we thought we knew who did it. The man we suspected was spending the boy's collection money. He was spending it here in town two days after Christmas.

"But we didn't have any proof of anything except the boy was dead."

"Was there an autopsy," I asked.

"Sure," said Kingdon, "accidental death, log rolled over on him, but it was wrong. Doc never performed a murder autopsy before, and to my knowledge the state police detective had never investigated a murder before."

The pieces of Shirley's clairvoyant puzzle were fitting together.

"Where was the body found?" I asked.

"Outside of town," said Kingdon, "near the Bangor and Aroostook Railroad tracks."

"Is that place called Cheney's?" I asked.

"No," he said. "Cheney's Grove, if that's what you mean, is a quarter-mile away."

If Kingdon were correct, the pieces of the psychic puzzle were coming together neatly, however one piece of the puzzle did not exactly fit.

With the comments of this newspaperman in mind, I realized that ESP was a logical target for skeptics. I knew the seriousness of Shirley's clairvoyance had been injured in the minds of many by Kingdon's analysis of it, which he had published in his paper. But, on the other hand, the blazing publicity of the case had extended her public. There must be those who had not committed themselves to personal beliefs. I shared Shirley's credo that ESP must be reported, reported either way, right or wrong. Shirley's burden was to learn the truth.

Neither was I convinced, not yet, anyway, that Shirley Harrison had been wrong. To clarify these points I interviewed detectives who had worked on the case.

Otis LaBree of LaBree Associates, Private Investigating, lives in Old Town, Maine.

In 1964, at the time of the autopsy, Otis had retired as a homicide investigator for the Maine State Police to be chief of police of Old Town. It was there that the State issued a statement which said: "As a result of this investigation [into the disappearance of Cyrus Everett] it can be stated that no evidence has been discovered to indicate that this death was otherwise than accidental."

Apparently, State's official position was that Cyrus had taken a short cut through the swamp, walked across the top of the log, and it rolled over on top of him.

Incensed at this opinion, the town manager of Fort Fairfield called Otis LaBree and asked him to come north and investigate the matter privately. This LaBree did, as I was to learn.

Early in winter, on November 24th, 1965, at a press conference at Fort Fairfield, LaBree released his conclusions.

"It's not accidental, it's a homicide," he told reporters. He said that Cheney's Grove is a short cut to nowhere. He said that the position of Cyrus Everett's clothes was inconsistent with those of a boy struggling to get free from the log. LaBree cited "head injuries" detected in a second autopsy report and concluded the newsboy had been robbed and beaten to death. He said that Cyrus' body had been dragged to its final resting place under the log.

LaBree mentioned Cheney's Grove by name as the marsh in which the body was found.

The psychic pieces of Shirley's puzzle had finally fit together.

Was Shirley Harrison's clairvoyant information correct? I asked LaBree.

"Mrs. Harrison's prediction was almost dead right," said the detective. "The boy was found in a swamp sometimes called Cheney's Grove." And under a heavy log. In fact, LaBree had called it by that name himself. He speculated that authorities would have had to use dynamite to free the youth's body from ice had it been searched for as she directed the winter the youth was lost.

"They would have found it easily," he said.

LaBree's outright defiance had led to the assignment of State Police Detective Camille Carrier to recheck the case.

After my conversations with LaBree, I returned to interview Shirley further. I learned that she had continued to work on the Cyrus Everett case at a friend's house. Notes had been taken, she said, and copies forwarded to a parapsychological investigator in Los Angeles, California.

It was then that State Police Detective Camille Carrier arrived at her house, said Shirley. Carrier, said Shirley, was amazed at the accuracy of her information as confirmed by LaBree.

Shirley told Camille Carrier that she had learned in her uncanny way that a person "who knew too much" about the murder of Cyrus Everett owned a pickup truck. That person was "considering doing away with himself," said Shirley. She urged Carrier to question him without delay.

Weeks later, a possible witness in the case was found in the cab of his pickup truck dead of asphyxiation. In the opinion of the detective, he had committed suicide.

The controversy about the murder of Cyrus Everett and its investigation lingers to this day. That story is not the purpose of this book.

What is, is the simple fact that Shirley Harrison's clear perception of the location of the boy proved accurate. Her strong feeling that he was indeed murdered proved to be the truth, he had been killed, as a second autopsy proved.

Again, the mystery of how she was able to achieve these insights remains a mystery. But it only increased our determination to probe further into other cases and eventually led to more probing interviews with Shirley Harrison herself. In her biography, the retelling of her life story, perhaps some of these shadows could be removed and light shed on the mysterious "how" of her unique abilities.

The Diamond Solitaire

Another facet of Shirley Harrison's psychic personality is revealed for us by her astounding ability to find lost objects. I learned that Shirley has been called upon countless times to locate not only such urgently needed items as car keys, but also to find children's toys, and even family pets. Shirley has pinpointed the hiding places of sentimental treasures such as a golden brooch containing human hair which had been a family heirloom for centuries. She has located deeds sequestered and then forgotten. She has described the resting places of wedding rings and directed the anxious owners to them. A file of letters from grateful neighbors attests to the unassuming generosity with which Shirley has given her clairvoyant powers and time.

For the most part, these have been simple, although equally outstanding problems for Shirley to solve. Other problems have proved more complex. One such case involved valuables worth millions.

This is the case attested to by criminologist Bruce Publicover, the second-generation owner of a Massachusetts-based security and detective agency with branch offices in Portland, Maine. So effective have the Publicover investigations proved that their agency has gained national and international fame not only in matters of security surrounding skyscraping office buildings, vast military installations and political intrigues, but also in matters concerning the individual client. Publicover's discretion and insight have become legendary in New England.

It is only because this case involving Shirley Harrison so astounded the detective, that he sought, at my request, to gain a release from his client. My purpose was to present it here as another example of Shirley's psychic abilities. This account is fully attested to by Bruce Publicover himself. The actual names have been omitted as a condition of permission to use this true case history. Its authenticity is verified by Bruce Publicover himself.

"What the story is about," related Bruce Publicover, sitting across a wide mahogany desk one sunny morning at the St. John Street office of the family firm's Portland branch, "is that we were hired by the executors of the estate of a woman who lived elsewhere in New England. She had died of cancer. Apparently, she was of a religious faith which forbade treatment.

"Her husband lived with her in a sizeable mansion with a staff of house and groundkeepers. They had one child, a daughter

"My information," said Publicover, "is that before the mother died she had a conversation with her daughter. It concerned jewelry the mother had hidden away. It was to be her daughter's."

The daughter, sensitive to her mother's wishes, read accurately the future conditional tense of her mother's promise. Respectful of her mother's faith which promised immortality not only in heaven but here on earth as well, and aware that people grow old only by deserting their ideals, the daughter did not ask for the location of the jewelry. That question would have implied a suspicion of her mother's impending death.

But, sensing her daughter's unspoken query, the mother answered it. She said her attendant, a woman in the family's employ, would deliver the purse of jewelry to her at the proper time.

After an agonizing illness, the mother died. Several weeks passed before the will was opened by the executors of the estate. In that interim, the daughter directed the attendant, an elderly woman of many years tenure with the family, to locate the jewelry for her. The daughter claimed her mother's authority to do so and she related her earlier conversation with her mother.

The attendant replied that her employer had a similar conversation with her regarding such a purse of jewelry. She had said that her daughter would know where it was. It was to be hers as a reward for many years of devoted service.

"The irony of this as they related it to me," said Publicover, "appeared to confound not only the daughter, but also the attendant. In any case, the purse was nowhere to be found. The old lady was by no means a solitary woman. Many had worked in the house and on the estate. Nurses, cooks, physicians, in addition to her husband, the attendant, and the daughter had visited her bedroom. But, no list of visitors to the mansion had been kept."

Moreover, Publicover found jewelry scattered about over her dressing tables, chairs and bed. He learned she had recently removed still more jewelry from safe deposit boxes and had brought it to her room. The staff had lost track of the exact dates certain pieces had been in the house, where it had last been seen and by whom.

The executors could not rule out the possibility that she had hidden the items. Consequently, they hired Publicover Security Service to resolve the mystery.

In their brief to the detective, they estimated the jewelry to be worth perhaps a quarter of a million dollars, but it was apparent that there was enough involved in the daughter's inheritance so that was not a major portion of it so far as money was concerned. In fact, the issue was basically a tax matter. The assignment given Publicover was to establish that these items, if not stolen, were lost and were not recovered; that in any case they were not in possession of the heirs.

Consequently, Bruce Publicover himself commenced to search the mansion room by room. He found the house cluttered. The old lady had kept everything. It appeared that over the years she had not so much as thrown away a letter. This was confirmed by the servants. She had piled and labelled her correspondence. Even broken objects such as dishes and vases, were placed in bags and labelled and stored. It was obvious that her possessions and the storing of them had been her principal preoccupation for many years.

Publicover learned from the servants that the jewelry had been in the old lady's possession a month or two before she died. At least, she had referred to it as if she had remembered where it was. He suspected that she had secreted it away personally. Therefore, it may not be far from her bed.

In fact, her doctors reported to him that she was not capable of travelling very far. Yet, he knew that she had a nurse and that she used a walker. He was to learn that there were times that, although physically impaired, she had not seemed to feel so. At these times, said the servants, she had seemed to move about freely, to climb stairs, to actually almost scamper over the grounds.

Consequently, the jewelry could be anywhere in the house or outside it. It was also revealed through Publicover's conversations with the staff that hiding things was a recurring motif in the old lady's conversation. It was another of her preoccupations, and she appeared to exult in the intrigue it engendered.

The detective searched the mansion with characteristic thoroughness, not excluding the attic.

There he found treasures that would have astounded Sinbad. He found racks of mink coats in brown paper bags. He found steamer trunks — no less than seven — full of Sterling silver. Although the coats and the silver were on a manifest provided by his clients, Publicover learned that the daughter had long ago forgotten about them. He found a portable writing table of intriguing uniqueness. He considered it a masterpiece of cabinetry and, of course, it was immediately suspicious to him.

The old lady, he learned, had been a carver of decoys. She had adapted a small summer house on the grounds into a woodworking shop.

Acting on instinct, Publicover disassembled the writing table. In it he found a secret compartment. In the compartment he found a box of gold coins. He made a note of the coins in his report to the executors.

As he proceeded to search the attic, he found that a portion of it was entirely filled with Christmas ornaments and presents. They were wrapped in ornamental paper, some of it hand-painted, and tied with ribbons. Some of the ribbons looked to be of handmade lace. The gifts were addressed with assurances of affection. Publicover realized that Christmas had been a season for which the old lady had spent many months preparing. Yet she had not given her gifts.

"Why?" he wondered. "Was it an eccentricity, a lapse of memory, an episode of senility?" Whatever the cause, she had withheld them. The detective realized that her behavior in hiding the jewelry and in misleading both her attendant and her daughter was not without precedent. Evidence for this observation lay all about him in the immense attic as tightly stocked with merchandise as the sales floor of a major department store.

Publicover observed, with characteristic understatement, that he was learning more about his client than was at first apparent.

For among the old lady's passions was an affection for cats. More than fifty cats had run unrestrained throughout the mansion. In the lower floors there were furnishings once beautiful. There were Oriental rugs and antique chairs, stained and broken. There were couches covered in embroidered upholstery, but ripped to tatters. The furnishings had been demolished. It was as if by decree. Some lay in shreds of gold and silver thread. All smelled of cats.

The detective searched carefully through this mansion, so vast and in such disarray, but he found no jewels.

It was at this point in the case that he contacted Shirley Harrison. He had first heard her speak at the exclusive Woodford's Club of which he was a life member. She had seemed to be logical and convincing in her description of ESP as a sixth sense. Her profound firsthand knowledge of her subject and her candor impressed the detective. It was clear to him that she had mastered the art of what entertainers call projection. She seemed to achieve an intimate one-to-one relationship with each member of her audience.

She had pointed out, as if personally to the rational criminologist, that intuitive knowledge, which she called ESP, had been measured. She had said that it was part of the scientific concepts of such thinkers as Einstein and Freud. She had told them at that meeting, that there was a project sponsored by the respected Menninger Foundation to determine if there was any connection between creative intuition and ESP ability. And, she had mentioned that the director of the project was the famed parapsychologist, Dr. Gardner Murphy, who had given the keynote address at her conference on ESP at a nearby university.

Creative intuition, as the detective had learned, was sometimes rewarding in his work, even after intelligent deliberation had convinced him that a solution was not possible. He knew that without it, had he proceeded by correct and commendable rules, he would have abandoned the cause. Naturally, he expected to utilize all police strategies, but also, he knew he could not look far in the dark.

Bruce Publicover concluded that Shirley Harrison's description of her powers was true to her own sense of reality. He felt he understood it. He asked her to help him find the purse of jewelry for his client.

Characteristically, Shirley said she would try, and that she would work on it and call him.

In the meantime, he continued with his investigation. He prepared to interrogate all the people associated with the house. He prepared to do financial checks and asset checks and to examine financial statements. He would discover if anybody had started to spend more money than their normal income would allow.

A few days later, Shirley telephoned. As if in jest, she asked the detective, "In your search of the house, did you also find some gold coins?"

The detective was astonished. He had not told her of the gold coins.

Shirley also remembers that conversation vividly. Here is her account of it.

"He seemed surprised when I mentioned gold coins. He had not mentioned them to me, but I had somehow seen them as I was concentrating on the jewelry. But, he did confirm that in his search for lost items, he had come across gold coins inside the secret compartment of a writing desk. These were the coins which I had seen in my ESP efforts," Shirley said.

The detective continued to search the mansion. In the living room there were bookshelves covering an entire wall. There were books also in the old lady's study and in her private sitting room and in her bedroom. There were hundreds of books to be searched.

There were also fireplaces to be pulled apart brick by brick. There were desks and tables to be dismantled and searched for hollow legs and secret compartments.

Publicover searched first in the bedroom. He remembered the jewelry was one of the last items the old lady had talked about. He guessed that she would relish the prospect of watching over its hiding place. He began to take down and leaf through every book to be sure it was not hollowed out. It was arduous work and he had been searching for weeks, so that when he got into nests of paper and cloth, nests wet and reeking of cats, he decided to leave instructions to the daughter to finish searching the books. In the presence of one of the heirs he called Shirley Harrison.

Perhaps, at this point, it is important to establish further the frame of reference and the attitude of Bruce Publicover toward Shirley Harrison. And the impression her revelations had made on the famed detective.

"In short," said the detective, "she made me a believer. May I remind you that I look at everybody and everything skeptically. It is my habit. Nothing is ever 100 percent. So that after she called me back, I went to my files and looked up the information I had given her. It was a letter. Some of the feedback I got from her could have been derived from the information in the letter.

"But she told me of additional items! In fact, she added to my list of jewelry I was retained to recover! I had not described the lady's companion, although I had told her that a staff existed. Her descriptions of specific people could not have come from me. 1 wanted very much to discover whether she had rehashed my information and given it back to me. She had not! There was information there that did not come from me.

"In my business," he continued, carefully explaining, "we take certain information and come up with possibilities. I don't think she could have done that.

"She did not talk in generalities. She was definite and accurate. She gave me specific items and locations and personal characteristics."

Publicover had called Shirley Harrison only after he had exhausted the best possibilities. Naturally, he cleared it with his clients, the trust people, before engaging Mrs. Harrison, for theirs was a business arrangement. He told his clients that Mrs. Harrison had an uncanny reputation among sources within his profession. He mentioned federal, state and local police. He said that although it was pretty whacky, he considered it to be worth a try.

He paid Shirley Harrison, although, in fact, he said she offered to do the work free.

"Like other people with whom I discussed the phenomenon of Shirley Harrison, I suspected that one of her strict rules was that she accept no money for her work. But to the contrary, I could not see why those seeking her services should deny her the means of subsistence. They should pay for her time, if nothing else."

The amount was $200. She did not ask for that, of course; neither did she refuse it. It was important to the detective that Shirley accept payment because, in the event her information proved accurate and he located the jewelry based on her information, she otherwise could be entitled to a finder's fee. It would be equal to a percentage. The detective's decision, after talking with the family's lawyers, was to pay for her time so that she would then have no claim to the jewelry should she find it. He and his attorneys decided that would be the neatest, cleanest, way to handle the matter.

To help summarize Shirley's information in his mind, the detective numbered her items of information.

"Shirley Harrison told me," he recalls, "that, 1: the jewelry was out of the house; 2: that it had been hidden behind books before being removed from the house; 3: she described the person removing the jewelry [this description is deleted by agreement with our source's client]. That description was a startling physical and psychological word portrait of a member of the staff. It was so clear and specific that I knew who it had to be, without mistake. 4: she described three items of jewelry which were not on my list from the executors."

This startled and puzzled the detective. He clearly remembered a passage from her lecture at Woodfords about her experiences from many years of ESP. Her exact words were: "When I finally fit that final puzzle into my information, I send it back repeatedly to the source of my information. If it is returned to me — ping-ping — with a feeling of confidence. . ." The detective recognized that Shirley's method of getting a hold on ESP was by relating one factor, confirming it, casting about over a field of information, then selecting items based on success, a "ping-ping", as she called it. This tracking process, she had said, required concentration. It was an intense process of asking and then reaffirming what she had learned.

"She read me her list of jewelry items," said Publicover. "There were eight items. My list contained only five items. Not only was there a diamond solitaire not on my list, but there were two more items." Her items alone, he estimated, would be worth perhaps $250,000.

Shirley told Publicover that the employee had taken the jewelry, that one of the items had been sold in Boston, that the employee had opened a bank account with the money, and that she still had other items.

To the detective that was most interesting. And then a few days later, the lawyers for the account called him. They added another item to his list. It was a diamond solitaire!

"I made careful notes at the time," Publicover insisted. "It is my habit."

He recalled another remark by Shirley. She had quoted her colleague, Dr. Gardner Murphy, who had, in the last year of his life, "warned me to preserve the precious evidence."

The detective knew well in matters such as these that after a while the eyewitnesses no longer remember what exactly had happened, and it is more convenient to assume they were deluded.

For that reason, perhaps, he wrote letters to confirm his telephone calls. He kept a carbon of his letters in a case file. They had proved useful. So had his notes of telephone conversations taken at the time.

The detective did not immediately abandon the search in his client's mansion for the purse of jewelry. But he soon postponed the house search and ordered periodic checks into the bank account of the employee Shirley described. It would be difficult, he knew, to conceal that amount of money for very long. He knew that most criminals justify their crimes, sometimes quite convincingly. Nevertheless, they sometimes act guilty even if they pretend not to feel so. When that amount of money starts getting spent, said the detective, it will leave a trail.

Yet, it would be a shame, said Publicover cynically, if the thief sold diamonds worth hundreds of thousands for a few dollars paid on the spot. If she had done so — or if she sold the items and did not spend the money — there would be no way to discover the sale by his bank account monitoring method. She may escape detection, but she would have wasted the jewels.

In this true account of that case of the missing jewelry, reconstructed here, the detective left the impression his investigation is not over; not until there is a final resolution.

However, he was able to report to his client that his search led to a reasonable belief that the jewelry was not in the house.

PART II

SHIRLEY'S
OWN STORY

Her First ESP Experiences

Many people accept ESP and psychic phenomenon at face value. Many others remain skeptics in varying degrees.

There are many people in New England, and around our country, and the world for that matter, who have psychic powers in varying degrees. Some are self-proclaimed psychics. They do not substantiate their claims with evidence. Others guard their privacy.

Shirley Harrison has protected her privacy and shunned the limelight. Nevertheless, she has appeared in the news periodically in connection with newsworthy cases and situations.

Shirley Harrison is a woman and a mother. She is a psychic with extraordinary powers. That can be accepted as fact because the facts have proved her uncanny and, at times, astounding abilities.

She has used her powers to find lost objects, lost children, lost aircraft, and in other more amazing cases, lost victims of violent crimes. Despite her unassuming character, she is undoubtedly a person of extraordinary abilities.

Tracking and tracing her abilities, documenting these cases with police, sheriff's department officials, FAA executives, private detectives, there remains little doubt that she had indeed done what she quietly has admitted to having done. The proof is in the reality, confirmed by these respected, honest, and forthright authorities.

The next question to be explored, and answered if possible, is perhaps the most difficult. Who is Shirley Harrison? How did she discover these powers? How does she do the astounding things she does do? And, what is it like, in personal terms, in inner feelings, to her when she is drawing upon these rare talents of psychic perception and power?

*It is time for a closer look at Shirley Harrison, the person.
This, is, after all, her story, her biography, and to a degree,
through her thoughts and comments, her autobiography.*

*To best understand Shirley Harrison, it requires the telling
of her personal story here.*

As a child, Shirley Baker Donham enjoyed the love of her
parents. In fact, she was surrounded by love in her rural New
England hometown of Island Falls, Maine.

Families were especially close. Parents, grandparents, relatives, neighbors, took time to tell stories to children, to read
aloud, to share experiences from their own youth. They took
time to pass on the true and dramatic, and sometimes heroic,
folklore of their ancestors who built their town.

Many of these stories contained stark tragedy and desperate
self-reliance. Some of these stories remained indelible in
young Shirley Donham's quick mind.

There is the story of her Danish 16-year old great-uncle who
trekked back home alone to his mother in New Brunswick
from the gold diggings of the West. He had been mining with
his father and they had, indeed, found gold, gold they en-
trusted to the boy to carry safely home where it was desperately needed by his mother. Over part of the 1,000-mile journey
home, the boy cut cross-country through woods rather than
risk the danger of pirates on the river. These pirates, so the
story tells, were more vicious than the wolves in the forest
which he feared not at all.

The boy trekked for weeks. When finally he staggered to
the end of his incredible journey, to his mother's door in New
Brunswick, he was starving to death, suffering from pneumonia. He died in his mother's arms. Yet in his pack he carried enough gold dust for his family to start a prosperous lum-
ber mill.

And there is the saga of Shirley's Yankee ancestor, Dr.
Isaac Donham, who, with a degree from Harvard Medical
School, pioneered north to the growing frontier town of Island Falls, a town of settlers who needed him desperately. He
practiced medicine — one of the first doctors in the Aroostook
territory — and prospered. When his son, Charles, grew to
early manhood, he enlisted in the Grand Army of the Republic
and went with it to Virginia. His father followed. He would

treat the wounded and be with his boy. However, fate decreed that his father would die, at Hampton Roads, Virginia, of exposure and exhaustion from treating the wounded on the battlefield, and the son returned home alone.

Of such stories is the history of Island Falls woven. Yet Shirley's ancestors were not only frontiersmen, miners and doctors; they were also newspaper editors and publishers, nurses, owners of hunting and fishing camps and schoolteachers.

Shirley also explored on a frontier where the very remarkable features of her mind made her outstanding.

In this chapter we learn of Shirley's first psychic experiences. It is a story remembered with crystal clarity by the person who lived it.

* * * *

As a child, I was in fact the surrogate mother of my younger sisters, Phyllis and Riva. Mother assigned them to my care. I took that job very seriously.

When I took them swimming, they were my first thought. We'd race out to a raft moored in 15 feet of clear lake water and gaze down at golden sand rippling and gleaming on the bottom. A favorite game was to dive for fistsful. Yet when I surfaced, my first concern was always, "Where is Phyllis? Where is Riva?" That was my first concern, all the time, summer and winter.

I took them to school. And always brought them home before dark.

It is not surprising, then, that my first psychic experience centered on one of them. It was about Phyllis, then eleven years old, the youngest.

This time I was spending a weekend away from my sisters. I was at the house of a friend of my age across town. We were listening to jazz records, making popcorn and fudge. We had been skiing, tobogganing and skating. On Saturday night our boyfriends of the moment came over and we danced. We took our dancing seriously. In fact, my boyfriend and I later won a jitterbug contest at Island Falls High School. On that particular Saturday night we cut a rug until the boys had to go home.

But on Sunday morning I began to feel uneasy. I was no longer the rugged, robust, skier, skater, dancer, Shirley Donham. I was uneasy. I was depressed by morbid thoughts I could not express. I had a feeling of dread. It got worse, and it began to center on Phyllis.

I ran home as hard as I could go. I burst into the front hall and confronted my mother. She was sitting reading in the living room.

"Where's Phyllis?" I demanded.

"She's gone down to the lake skating."

"You should not have let her go." I burst into tears.

Mother looked at me serenely and said, "Shirley she's a fine skater. You taught her yourself. She's with a crowd of young people. The ice is safe. They've been skating there all winter. What is wrong with you, dear? You look a little upset."

"You shouldn't have let her go," I insisted.

"I have no bad feelings," said mother.

Bewildered, distraught, I paced from window to window waiting, waiting, waiting the rest of the day for Phyllis to come home. I knew she was in danger.

By 5 o'clock it was dark. An hour later I heard a car stop out front. I rushed into the hall. I swung open the door just as two boys carried Phyllis up onto the porch. She was bandaged from ear to ear. She was deathly white. Yet the boys assured me, and they assured my mother, that Phyllis would be all right.

There had been an accident. They had been to the hospital. Doctor Swett said that Phyllis needed rest. She had been badly injured.

We finally pieced the story together: As it came on dusk they had skated in a wild, racing, free-for-all back to the landing at the head of the lake. One of the boys had a car. They would all pile in and ride to town. But the car was stuck. Phyllis, exhuberant, strong and capable, willing to help, clattered to the rear of the car and pushed hard, straining and sliding. She crashed down on her skates in the snow. Her neck fell across the sharp edge of the license plate. It cut her throat. She was bleeding badly.

One of the boys in the group that evening was Joe Sleeper, a Boy Scout. He acted fast and with self-confidence; with practiced method, he probed with his thumb for the pressure points in Phyllis' neck. He stopped the bleeding which by then was horrifyingly apparent to all the skaters.

Holding his hands in place, holding pressure against her artery, Joe helped Phyllis into the car. The other children pushed like desperate survivors. They started the car onto the road.

Half an hour later at the Island Falls Hospital, Dr. Swett, our family doctor, treated the cut. He said Joe Sleeper had saved the life of my sister Phyllis. He stitched and bandaged the deep cut.

As I listened to this story of what had happened to my baby sister, my sickness seemed to vanish. Phyllis would be all right. Her life had been saved. Yet she had been in terrible danger, danger I had somehow known!

That's why I was filled with anxiety about her. I knew! My whole being told me Phyllis was in trouble even before the accident happened. I knew of it, yes, even though I did not foresee that actual accident in detail. My dreadful foreboding had told me it would happen.

I confessed this to my mother.

"Maybe you have second sight," she answered matter-of-factly. "Grandmother Jeppson had it."

My mother admitted it. So premonitions were possible. I was proud to be like my Danish great-grandmother if that were to be the explanation of this event, my first touch of ESP in my life.

*　　*　　*　　*

The psychic experience of her sister Phyllis' critical accident mystified Shirley. Fortunately, in those childhood years, nothing so ominous as Shirley's psychic experience with her younger sister was ever to come through via clairvoyance to her again, yet there were little things, "minor incidents," as Shirley called them. There was the time she said to her friend from New York: "When you fell off your tricycle at age 6, you broke your leg and were in a cast for three months . . ." and it proved to be all too true. Her friends were amazed.

Shirley never did the "Oh, you're going to get a letter, or go on a long trip, or I see a tall, dark, handsome man," stuff.

"Forget that foolishness," said Shirley. She was a determined, curious, daring and dared, teenager. On one occasion when the ice went out of Pleasant Pond one spring, Shirley's friends dared her to be the first to go in the water. "I pulled on my bathing suit," said Shirley, "and plunged in. The ice was tinkling around me. It was May 5th!"

Another favorite teenager trick was stealing corn and chickens and potatoes for a cookout. "That was the height of daring-do for our crowd," said Shirley. "We loved that kind of mischief." Once she and her friends stole two laying hens — from a long-suffering relative. They cleaned them and roasted them, but they proved so tough in the eating they put them in shoe boxes and buried them and held a service.

"Another time," said Shirley, "we house partied at a camp for all girls with a chaperone and at another camp down the lakeshore the boys partied, also with a chaperone, and we had a marvelous time." Those were happy days. "We had few temptations," said Shirley. "Drugs? Absolutely not. We didn't even smoke cigarettes.

"I was president of the Loyal Temperance Union when I was 11 years old and delivered a paper on the evils of alcohol and cigarettes at a convention in nearby Houlton."

When Shirley graduated from Island Falls High School and went on to Ricker College, she found life strict. In fact, she was restricted to campus for two weeks merely for going downtown with a boy for an ice cream soda after a basketball game without permission.

While in high school Shirley attended Christian Endeavor every Sunday night. "I don't recall," said Shirley, "any mention in the church service or in Sunday school of the metaphysical nature of divine knowledge." There was one exception that Shirley recognized in those early years; that was the Easter Sunday service.

The words were, "though ye die, yet shall ye live . . . if it were not so would not I have told you?" Shirley found that statement believable then and now.

In Island Falls, the Catholic and the Baptist and the Congregational churches sometimes had a combined meeting. Shirley attended one midnight Mass in which a Catholic played the organ and a Congregationalist sang the Ave Maria.

"Mother said that we did not judge people by their color,"

said Shirley, "or by their religion or by their wealth, but by what they were personally as human beings.

"She was a wonderful mother. When we were small she sat outside our bedroom door nearly every night and read to us until we fell asleep. As a family we read constantly. Books were everywhere. Mother said that while we were not wealthy in material things, we were rich in the things nobody could take from us — good books, good music and many friends."

Shirley had a close relationship with her father. He was a hunting and fishing guide and to Shirley his life seemed not much different than an extended boyhood. He affirmed by the way he treated Shirley, that a woman could handle a canoe or a fishing rod as well as any man. Shirley and her father shared many days on Mattawamkeag Lake and in the pine and birch filled woods of northern Maine.

One night about midnight, Shirley's father rushed into the girls' bedroom and told them to get up quickly and dress and come with him. He led them out to the river where immense sheets of blue ice gleaming in the moonlight were grinding and tearing away the bank and climbing on top of themselves, crashing and submerging and thrusting up again. The ice, said Shirley, was piling up in the middle of the river threatening to carry away the bridge. It was not only a fantastic sight, there was a deep, thunderous, roar that seemed to fill the night. The ice was going out of the river a month earlier than usual, loosened by a warm rain. Her father, said Shirley, watched the ritual of nature with awe, as she did.

He loved nature, said Shirley. He took her with him on countless woods rambles. In the woods, said Shirley, he would stop suddenly and point to a clump of trees. "I'd look, too. It would be a fox or a deer," said Shirley. "We'd watch it together, sometimes for half an hour. Father seemed to move without a sound in the woods. I tried to do the same."

She remembers river trips in his canoe or through the woods on snowshoes. At lunchtime they would scoop a hole in the snow and build a fire. They would boil coffee and eat bacon and biscuits. "That was his exclusive diet in the woods," said Shirley, "and while we were feasting, he'd tell me stories. Oh, I loved him."

*   *   *   *

Every Sunday of Shirley's youth, she went to the Donham farm after church. There they made homemade ice cream, and popped corn in the cellar in the furnace with all of the family children seated around the open furnace door. They chopped ice for ice cream, hacking it off the pond, carrying it into the kitchen in a burlap bag. They took turns turning the crank of the ice cream freezer.

"It was always a feast," said Shirley. Her father provided venison and white perch and trout, partridge and wild duck stuffed with rice. In the spring they had fiddlehead greens, the young sprouts of wild ferns.

For dessert the children would sometimes make themselves sheepskins. They poured thick maple syrup made on the farm into the snow. It congealed and the children rolled it up and ate it. "The Indians used to make it," said Shirley. "It was delicious, but we children thought we were deprived because we couldn't have store-bought cake from the A & P."

At these Sunday dinners, the family reminisced and played their wind-up Victrola. Music was important to them. They listened to Caruso singing. Shirley's father would sing along with him. "These family gatherings were a warm and wonderful part of my childhood," remembered Shirley.

* * * *

Her great-grandfather on the maternal side of the family was a prosperous merchant in Denmark, in Copenhagen. "I remember grandmother, Karen Johnson, telling me," said Shirley, "that she went to school with a countess.

"Karen Johnson fell in love with my grandfather," said Shirley, remembering her grandmother's stories of their emigration to North America. "But the marriage was not approved. Her parents thought she had married beneath her. She defied her parents and followed her husband to Canada. Later she came to Maine."

Shirley's mother was their first child. Shirley was born in Island Falls in a Victorian house with a turret and a round bay window. The house stands there still on Sewall Street.

The trip to America from Denmark had not been an easy one, Karen Johnson had told Shirley. Neither was their rough life on a frontier farm easy.

Shirley was soon to learn that her own life was going to demand all of her resourcefulness also.

* * * *

At Ricker College, Shirley was an A student. She played on the varsity basketball team, was co-editor of the college paper, accompanist for the glee club. She loved college, the challenge, the friends and the chance to read and learn. But her father, although he loved her, was unable to make more than a bare living for his family as a guide and trapper. The Depression had hit hard. And at the end of Shirley's first college year, she was forced to apply personally for a scholarship. She asked for an appointment with the president and stated her need.

"You're an excellent student, Miss Donham," Shirley remembers him saying, "but all our scholarships are for men."

Shirley recalls that this was the first time she had ever felt discriminated against because she was a woman. She was forced to leave school. And took a job for a year as a bookkeeper in a small business firm in Portland.

"Looking back on those months," says Shirley, "I realize my employer was very patient with me. There was not a moment at that job when I did not want to be back either in Island Falls or in college."

* * * *

In 1942, she married a young man from Pennsylvania, Mike Harrison. They had first met at Mattawamkeag Lake in northern Maine when she was nine and he was eleven. "I resolved," said Shirley, "to devote myself entirely to my husband and then to my children."

Shirley's psychic powers surfaced time and again during those early married years. The young couple had moved to Philadelphia. Several of their friends were FBI agents; one of them having married a high school classmate of Shirley's. She knew details about a case they were working on. It was a highjacking scheme which had been infiltrated by the agents and soon would be stopped when the thieves were arrested. Shirley gave the address of the warehouse where the stolen goods were hidden, the names of the criminals, the names of other agents on the case. The FBI men later confided to her that everything she had told them that night was true.

It was obvious to Shirley, to her husband, to her friends, that hers were no ordinary powers. She could not deny them. Nor could they.

Their first child was born prematurely. While it was in the hospital, Shirley and Mike rode the train north to Island Falls. Their plan was to take advantage of the weeks the baby was cared for in the hospital to visit Shirley's parents. On their return, Shirley had another clairvoyant experience.

When she and Mike arrived in Boston on the return trip, they were required to transfer stations to continue south.

"I do not want to take the train," Shirley remembers telling Mike. "We must go by bus."

Mike obediently turned in his tickets and they took a taxi to the bus station and continued on to Philadelphia. They learned later that the train on which they had seats had derailed in Providence, Rhode Island.

Other premonitions surfaced in Shirley's psychic life. "I knew without doubt," she remembers, "that my baby would not come home."

So certain was she of this tragedy that she did not open the boxes of baby clothes sent by her family. When the baby died, Shirley was not shocked, she remembers. She had known it to be inevitable. "I knew also," said Shirley, "that my sensitivity could not help my child. If I were able to somehow know things, terrible things, I was not always able to protect those involved."

She had not protected Phyllis, her sister, from her near-fatal accident while skating. And although she had perhaps prevented Mike and herself from taking a train destined to derail that night, she had not saved the life of her first baby.

"A few weeks after my baby died, I had an experience which would alter my life forever. I had gone to bed and was lying in the dark unable to sleep. I was still struggling with the grief and the sense of loss. I felt utterly alone. I thought, 'I must get over this and go on.' Suddenly, I felt — although I saw nothing — surrounded by warmth and a golden light. I felt a presence. With it, a feeling of such love and comfort that I cannot find words to describe it. For a few brief moments I felt attuned to a higher being. There was a sense of perfect communion, of complete understanding.

"Then gradually the warmth, the light, the presence faded away. I remember thinking, 'Don't go. Stay.' But it was gone, and with it my feelings of hopeless grief and despair. I was still saddened by the death of my baby but not in the same way. I have never forgotten those moments. They gave me an unshakable faith in a divine creator.

"Materialistic psychologists dismiss these experiences as reactions to traumatic stress. I do not agree.

"My friend Hilda Ives described a similar experience to me. Here is her account as I remember it. Hilda had lost her husband in the flu epidemic following World War I. She was left with four children, one a baby in arms. After months of anguish, one day she entered her house, took off her coat and collapsed full length on the floor. She said to herself, I can't live. I can't live.

"Then she sensed a divine presence. Her experience was exactly like mine. The warm golden light. The sense of being surrounded by a living presence. She later became a fine Congregational minister. She served the community with dedication helping scores and scores of people. She would sit and talk with a suicidal person night after night. She went into court with the poor to plead their cases. She brought them clothes when they had none. She went to Belgium with the Red Cross. She was sent to India on a world health and peace mission. She wrote a book about her life, *All In One Day*."

*　*　*　*

In June, 1943, Mike was drafted and sent as a medic to Burma. Shirley went home to Island Falls. She would wait for him there, among her family. She began to question and experiment with her psychic abilities encouraged by her friend Dr. Clyde Swett.

For two years Shirley practiced ESP as if it were a skill to be developed. It was an intellectual exercise. Dr. Swett had studied hypnosis at McGill University in Montreal. To him, Shirley's potential was obvious. In fact, her clairvoyance astounded all who witnessed it and all in whom she confided.

It was with Dr. Swett that the young Shirley first experienced the astonishing mysteries of the Ouija.

First Ouija Board
Discoveries

Another landmark in Shirley Donham's psychic sensitive development was her introduction to hypnosis and to controlled experiments with psychic sensitivity by her family doctor, Dr. Clyde I. Swett. That episode in her life opened new horizons to her own unique abilities. The time was 1944. She still recalls that period vividly as she does the other significant plateaus of her developing psychic consciousness.

Doctor Swett was our family doctor. Shirley remembers. He had studied at McGill University in Montreal and he used hypnosis in his practice. He had hypnotized me several times just for fun. I was so attuned to hypnosis that he gave me the post-hypnotic suggestion that only a medically trained person may hypnotize me again, ever in my life.

A few years later, my sister Riva worked for Dr. Swett in the hospital in Island Falls. He taught her hypnosis also, and she, too, became adept at it. If she had a terrible day at the hospital or, if, in the middle of the afternoon, Riva were absolutely exhausted, she did what Dr. Swett taught her to do. She pressed a point on her shoulder and went into a brief hypnotic state. It rejuvenated her. She said it was almost as good as a night's rest.

One day Dr. Swett hypnotized Riva. It was mid-summer, hot, in the 90s. Dr. Swett waved a glass of water under Riva's nose. "Wouldn't you like this glass of cold beer?" he asked. "It's such a hot day."

"No."

"Why not?"

"Because I'm on duty."

That incident showed me that human will still functions even under hypnosis.

Riva and I became more aware and excited about exploring the new consciousness we were developing with Dr. Swett.

And then he gave us a Ouija board for a birthday present. "Try it," he said. "See what happens."

Just for fun, Riva and I sat down knee to knee. We read the directions on the counter.

Place the OUIJA talking board upon the laps of two persons facing each other, lady and gentleman preferred.

Place OUIJA MYSTERIOUS MESSAGE INDICATOR in center of Ouija talking board resting fingers with the least possible pressure upon the mysterious message indicator, allowing it to move freely over OUIJA talking board in all directions.

Questions may be asked and in from one to five minutes the mysterious message indicator will commence to move, at first slowly, then faster. As it passes over Ouija talking board each letter of a message is received as it appears through the transparent window covered by the message indicator.

2nd — Care should be taken that one person only ask questions at a time so as to avoid confusion.

3rd — To obtain the best results it is important that the persons present should concentrate upon the matter in question and avoid other topics. If you use it in a frivolous spirit, asking ridiculous questions, laughing over it, you naturally get undeveloped influences around you.

We placed our hands on the indicator . . .

Riva melodramatically said . . . "Who is the Ouija?"

To our astonishment, the board seemed to come alive. Our hands whipped into action. The indicator under our hands spelled "the Ouija board is a plaything for fools . . . and you are fools."

All the hairs on my arms stood up straight. And then I asked the Ouija, "Who are you?"

"A higher form of life."

And then it stopped moving. I wanted to explore more. I didn't believe what had just happened. Riva must have been thinking the same thing because she commanded, "I say, move this indicator. We are tired of waiting here."

To our astonishment once again the Ouija moved.

It said, "You do not give the commands. We are in command here. We won't answer you until we are ready."

And then it said, "Be gone ye mortals!"

That was all. Riva and I held our hands on the board for another hour, but with no results. We reported our experiences to Dr. Swett.

"Very interesting," he said. "Try it again in a few days . . . when you feel like it."

Another time we sat down with the Ouija board, Riva and I together, knee to knee as before, our hands on the indicator. I'll never forget what happened.

We got a communicator who said he was a young French boy. He had died in the war. He lived in Marseille.

We asked how he was killed.

He said he was in the French underground resistance. He was blowing up bridges, blowing up ships. He said they were having a meeting in a basement and somebody threw a bomb through the window. He said his name was François.

This absolutely astounded us. I took notes. I showed them to Dr. Swett.

"Interesting," he said. "Keep on experimenting."

Then a friend of my mother's — both were amused at our game — said, "Why don't you ask the Ouija to find my snapshots? They are of my grandson. They are the only ones I have."

It was during World War II. Film was scarce. You could buy only so many packages at a time and then it took a long while to have them developed.

"Would you ask the board, please?" said mother's friend. Why not?

Riva and I went to the board again.

"Tell her to look where the furs are kept," said the board. "The furs, the furs," it repeated. "The fur piece that she wears!"

So we called her and told her our Ouija news. "Oh, my mink stole," she said. "My Christmas present. My children gave it to me."

She rushed to the hall where her stole was hanging in the closet. She looked in the little pocket. Nothing. No photographs. She was disappointed.

A few days later, she was cleaning another closet. This one was in the bedroom. She pulled out a box in which, incidentally, her stole had come from the store in Bangor. She lifted the cover and there they were! Her photographs of her first grandchild.

She called my mother. "Of course," she said. "It's so obvious. My fur came in that box. That is where the furs are kept!"

After that incident, we used our Ouija ability to locate many small missing objects. Dr. Swett was delighted. I suspect my mother was secretly amused.

Only a few friends were aware of our ESP project. Maurine, my best friend in school, had married. Her husband Hal said, "Don't you think this is a little too much. It's time to admit you are playing a game on us."

We said, "Yes. But it's fun. We're tired of playing bridge and going to the movies."

"All right," said Maurine. "If you're so interested in your Ouija board, here is our problem. We need a washing machine. We have a new baby. Where are we going to find a washing machine, used or otherwise?"

So Riva and I asked the Ouija, "Where can Maurine find a washing machine?"

The answer came back promptly.

[Shirley has requested that the actual name be withheld]

"A man in Oakfield has one he will sell you."

"Oh, is that so?"

"Yes, his wife died a few months ago. He now has a housekeeper and he'd like to sell the washing machine. Why don't you call him?"

Hal went straight to the telephone and cranked it. That's the way you rang up in those days. He called the name of the man in Oakfield that the Ouija suggested."

Oakfield is an even smaller town than Island Falls about 15 miles north on Route 2.

Gladys connected Hal with a real person!

He handed me the phone.

"I understand you have a washing machine for sale!" I said.

"Why yes," the man replied. "I do have a washing machine for sale; at least I've been thinking about selling it. My wife died a few months ago. Now I have a housekeeper. She wants me to keep it, but I want to sell it. She can do what little laundry we have in her own machine."

"My friends do need a washing machine over here," I said.

"Oh, I think we can do business," he said.

And then he said, "By the way. I haven't advertised this machine yet. How did you know about it?"

"Oh, someone told me. However, I don't remember who!"

Dr. Swett was delighted with this new development.

"You are getting factual information," he said. "You are getting names. Not only did you know his wife died, you knew the name of the town where she lived. You have the ability, Shirley," he said. "Your mind can transcend matter."

I was encouraged, ESP became a great interest for me. I began to read the books Dr. Swett loaned me. I read William James, Joseph Banks and Louisa Rhine. Dr. Swett also loaned me Edgar Casey's *There Is A River*. There were many more. I read everything I could get my hands on. In fact, I read everything on parapsychology in the Island Falls library.

We often would enjoy ourselves with the Ouija board. But, like most people, we could not understand it or explain what happened when we used it.

Actually, we assumed that other people also could learn things from the Ouija. If we could learn from it, then, logically, so could they.

Not until years later did I realize that there seems to be a direct relationship between success with a Ouija board and a person's psychic abilities. As a matter of fact, during my first experience with the Ouija back there in Island Falls with my sister, Riva, I did not even know what a psychic sensitive was. I had never heard the phrase.

Dr. Swett told us that serious students of parapsychology did not use the Ouija board for a prolonged period of time. Neither did they use it for frivolous attempts at communication with purported spirits. He warned us that we must guard against the inclination to use the board to express our own individual decisions in life and he said this tendency could result in serious psychological damage to us . . . He warned that as a device for guiding and forecasting the future the Ouija could be totally unreliable.

Even when my sister and I reported to Dr. Swett that spe‑ cific names and places we had learned from the Ouija had turned out to be correct, Dr. Swett continued to warn us. False information can be mixed in with accurate fact, he said. Only information that can be checked out should be accepted. I have always followed his advice. I evaluate every ESP experience objectively and critically.

The Boston Strangler

*In our interviews there were times when Shirley told me
of her psychic experiences in chronological order just as she
experienced them. I was able to document many of these
experiences by tracking down and interviewing first-person
witnesses and public officials she named in her narratives. At
other times, Shirley subjected me to a rapid-fire flow of consciousness. I transcribed our tapes and returned them to
Shirley for clarification. Together we developed this material
in a logical manner or pattern that is expected of a reporter,
writer, author. I have no psychic powers, and had I not
transcribed what I did not at first understand, I would have
missed much that is significant in the flow of Shirley's
thoughts as she actually expressed them.*

*Here we learn of still more psychic police work as Shirley
tells of her role in the notorious Boston Strangler case. Once
again, witnesses have provided letters attesting to Shirley's
clear and accurate recollections.*

*Here also, we learn of psychic dreams shared by Shirley's
children. We learn of still another incident of precognition;
this time so precise was Shirley's clairvoyant foretelling that
she was able to save the life of her friend and mentor,
Ruth Hyde.*

*Here, as Shirley tells the story, we travel to Italy on a
psychic quest to pinpoint the location of a priceless manuscript
in the ruins of the ancient city of Herculaneum.*

*Here, in this section, are Shirley's thoughts and memories.
They are in the words of the sensitive herself, straightforward
to read.*

I learned of the next victim of the Boston Strangler from
the Ouija. It happened in New York. I had attended a conference of parapsychologists. After the day's meetings we all

went to the apartment of Dr. Bill Erwin to chat. Stanley Krippner, Norman McGhee, Jean Snyder, Zelda Suplee were all there; a learned group in the field of parapsychology.

They all wanted to see me perform: "Here's a psychic." "Let's see what we have been writing so much about." "Show us how you do it." "Will you demonstrate the Ouija board?"

Yes, I would try.

I drew a Ouija board because it facilitates the flow of words. Really, it is just a sensitive's typewriter; just a device, a tool, no more. I proceeded to mark all the letters of the alphabet and at the bottom, "YES" and "NO" on a piece of cardboard.

I concentrated. After many questions from the group and after getting names which seemed relevant to those in the audience and which were truly uncanny, came these words. They rang clear. I repeated them out loud. "On Boston street there walks a man. He is mad. He lusts after a woman. He follows her beneath the street light. He is going to kill her. You must stop him. He kills with a stocking or a scarf."

Then somebody in the room remarked that the language seemed archaic. Another screamed, "My God, the Boston Strangler!"

Was that true? I asked the Ouija.

The Ouija answered, "Yes. He is called that. You must stop him."

"Where does he work?" I asked.

"He works in a great hospital," said the Ouija. "He pushes elderly men in wheelchairs. He shaves them. He puts on their bathrobes."

"Is he married?" I asked.

"Yes, sometimes separated. He has children."

"What does he look like?"

"Dark hair."

"The girl, the victim?"

"She is a nurse."

"Where is he going to kill her?"

"On Charles Street near the Charles Street jail."

This was astounding, terrifying news. It was clear and detailed. Bill Erwin relayed it to Jess Stearn, the novelist, whom I learned got in touch with George Frazier, the Boston Herald columnist. Bill asked particularly if police could be stationed on Charles Street near the jail. This was in the fall.

I returned to Maine. A week later, I went down to Duke for testing with Bill Roll. Then I came back to Maine to life as usual.

Around the first week in January at midnight or very early in the morning, the phone rang. A voice, frenzied, said, "Oh, Mrs. Harrison, it's happened! It's happened! He killed her where you predicted! It's the Boston Strangler!"

I was groggy and then I was horrified.

"It was where you said," the voice continued. "The street and block are those you predicted. Do you realize the mathematical odds against this being mere guesswork? This is incredible, Shirley. You could not have put the idea into the killer's head because your Ouija experience in New York was not made public."

It was George Frazier. He asked me to come down to Boston immediately for questioning by detectives.

I said, yes, of course. I would do what I could. I went to Boston by bus because of bad flying weather. There was a terrible blizzard, but I got there.

George Frazier and two detectives met me at the bus station and we drove directly to a hotel. They registered me under an assumed name. We began questioning.

First, they asked me to look at pictures of the murder scene and of the body of the girl. But before I looked at pictures, I told the detectives and George that I got information that the murderer urinated on the floor.

"She could not have known that," said one of the detectives, "because it was not printed in the papers. Could you tell us more?"

I looked at the photographs. It was hideously apparent that the murderer had a terrible rage against women. I would do what I could to stop this mad murderer.

First, I reminded the detectives of the information I had learned from the Ouija in New York several months previously. The murderer worked in a hospital taking care of old men. He pushed them in wheelchairs. He shaved them and put on their bathrobes. He has children and he is sometimes separated from his family. He has dark hair.

The detectives said my information was in their notes, but they desperately needed the name and residence of the murderer.

I would do what I could. Our questioning session lasted into the evening. They concentrated on two questions: Who is he? Where is he?

I must tell you that I do not remember what I told those detectives that day. I do remember that when they left I was so exhausted I fell across the bed fully clothed and slept through to morning.

That was when George Frazier called again. He said he and two detectives were in the lobby. Would I ride through the streets of Boston with them?

Yes, of course. It was still snowing. The car slewed about. Once, the detectives had to push it out of a drift.

"If you have any impressions as we drive, would you tell us?" asked Frazier. I held a pen poised to write on a legal pad in my lap as thoughts appeared or came to me. I was concentrating on my impressions, blocking out all else. I was doing my utmost to help these men prevent another murder. Yet nothing happened.

But then, suddenly, the pen began to move. It whirled, violently tearing and ripping the pad. It scribbled erratic lines. It seemed to me as if the pen was trying to express horror!

"Something!" I said. "Right here!"

"For good reason!" Frazier exclaimed. "This is the building where the murder was committed."

George Frazier told me later that a Dutch psychic had also been called in on the case and that when he reached that spot, just as I had, he demanded to be driven away. He had screamed that he was choking and he had called it an evil place. There was no question about that in my mind.

That is all I know about my role in the case of the Boston Strangler. The police told me nothing. I suspect they do not want it known that they have used psychics. It is not quite the thing to do. Therefore, the psychic herself is the last person to be told if her information proved helpful.

They were kind enough to pay my bus and hotel expenses. But I did not ask for a fee and was not paid one. I have never asked for a fee for anything I ever did. Not ever.

The Feldspar Mine

Shirley's account of her accurate precognition in the Boston Strangler case is confirmed by documentation. It is proved. Shirley has had other similar testings of her psychic powers. She remembers them vividly. In fact, some of them are landmark cases in her own exploration of her clairvoyance. This case of the Feldspar Mine is told here in Shirley's own words as she recounted it.

This case I call the "Feldspar Mine" continues to intrigue me. I received a telephone call one evening. It was from an attorney who said he needed information. His investigation of a missing man had led nowhere. I said that when all else fails, people call me. He admitted that to be the case.

He asked, "What happened to Fred McIntyre?" Just like that, out of the blue. "He has been missing for 25 years," he told me.

He gave the date of his disappearance. That was all. I said I'd try. So I sat down with my pad and pencil and prepared to do automatic writing. My pencil wrote: "Look in the mine."

What mine?

"An old feldspar mine."

What happened?

"They killed him. They took him in a northerly direction from the house and they put him in a mine."

Why?

"They were fighting over a game of cards. They didn't mean to kill him, but they did."

The next day the lawyer called back and asked — I could detect doubt in that voice — "Do you have anything for me?"

I said, "A little. Look for an old feldspar mine north of the house. It's not far away."

The lawyer said the subject was not a miner. He was a woodsman. The lawyer sounded discouraged but he was persistent. "I'll go out there," he said. "I know where he lived. Maybe I can find somebody who remembered him. Who knows? I don't know of any mines in this area."

In four hours he called back. He was excited. He said every hair on his head was standing up. Not only had he found an old-timer who remembered Fred McIntyre, but who also directed him to an old feldspar mine. It was a few hundred yards north of the house. The old man also remembered when Fred disappeared.

A week later we drove to the site. There, in a northerly direction from the McIntyre house, through a field and into a grove of pine trees was the feldspar mine. It was full of water.

The lawyer said my information was intriguing; that it was in fact uncannily accurate. Although there were no financial resources to drain the quarry, he was satisfied in his mind that my information accounted for the disappearance of Fred McIntyre.

Then he explained that his client was Fred's wife. She wanted to marry again. However, she was a devout Roman Catholic and she must have some assurance that her husband was dead. The lawyer offered to give her priest my information and to confirm that to our best available knowledge her husband was dead.

His client married with a clear conscience.

A Curious Skeptic

As Shirley's feats of ESP were proved to be true in real life, she was increasingly sought after. Many wanted to see for themselves if she could do what they had heard she could do, if she was in fact a true sensitive. Shirley's attitude toward her questioners was tolerant and understanding. She gave freely of her time. She would do her best. She did not blame her questioners for being curious. She was curious herself. Here she relates one of these intimate encounters.

One day a friend came to visit me. She was a total skeptic, but she was curious. She said, "What is it you do, you know, when you do that?"

I said, "Shall I try it for you?"

She said, "You know I don't believe in that, not at all."

I said, "That doesn't matter to me. We are friends. I'm not out to convert people. I'm not a missionary. You have your opinion. I have mine. I'm very open-minded about ESP. I have not made any judgments. I'm merely trying to find out what it is."

I placed a pad of paper in front of me and I took my pencil in hand and I waited. Nothing for a while: a few minutes. Then finally my hand wrote her name.

Then my hand wrote, "This is your mother."

My friend's mother had died. I knew that.

My friend said, "Oh, I don't believe that."

"Eunice," my hand wrote, "Don't you believe me?"

"No."

"I'll prove that I am your mother."

She "told" us several things pertinent only to Eunice and

her mother, but one was this: "Take off your wide wedding band and show Shirley my ring hidden beneath it."

Eunice turned white. She took off her own wide wedding band and there under it was the wire-thin gold band which had belonged to her mother.

"You couldn't see it," she said. "You couldn't know it was there . . ."

Herculaneum Search

Shirley has spent many hours, days and years devoting her ESP to helping others. Rarely was she supported by those who asked for help. One notable exception was Ruth Hyde the woman who became Shirley's mentor, who helped Shirley organize and orchestrate their conference in parapsychology at the University of Maine, a conference which was the first of its kind in northern New England. It was Ruth whose life Shirley may have saved when, in obediance to a precognitive feeling of doom associated with the trans-Atlantic flight Ruth was booked to fly, warned her to change her reservations.

Shirley and Ruth were to undertake another search together, this time it was an archeological expedition. Here is Shirley's story of Ruth and the letters at Herculaneum.

I met Ruth Hyde at a meeting where I was speaking. I said to the group, "There is someone here whose name is Ruth. I have a message for her. Jack wants to speak to her. He wants to tell her that his book is not finished and he wants her to find someone to finish this book. The book is about Paul."

There was no response from the audience. I went on with my lecture on ESP. Days — weeks — later, a car rolled into my driveway and a lovely woman got out to greet me. She took my hand and said, "I want to help you."

"Whatever for?" I asked. "Because you have a great gift," she said, "and you must use it. My name is Ruth and my husband was Jack and he was dedicated to his book about Paul the Apostle, a book he was not able to finish before he died."

She told me she had had a deep interest in ESP ever since her college years at Pine Manor in Wellesley, Massachusetts.

The head mistress there, said Ruth, was Helen Temple Cooke who openly discussed with her friends and her students her belief in ESP.

In fact, she was a psychic herself. She told her students of her many extraordinary experiences. She was also a disciple of the great psychologist, William James. The friendship between Ruth and Helen Cooke continued long after Ruth graduated from Pine Manor, and so did the influence of the teacher. Helen Cooke was to have a strong influence on the life of her student.

Later when Ruth married a young Congregational minister, John Hutchinson Hyde, she found a life partner who shared this deep interest. Together, they read and researched all kinds of psychic phenomenon. They met Dr. S. Ralph Harlow, professor of religion at Smith College, and with him spent many hours discussing psychic phenomenon and its potential for proof of survival after death. Dr. Harlow wrote a book still very much read. Its title: *A Life After Death.*

In Ruth Hyde's mind, ESP, psychic phenomenon and a deep, unshakable religious faith were inseparable, as they were *all* of the human spirit. Her studies led her to Duke University where she met with Dr. J. B. Rhine and his wife and colleague, Dr. Louisa Rhine.

When I expressed my doubts about going into parapsychological research, Ruth replied, "You must do it. We will find a way." And we did. The Research Association for Parapsychological Study was a result of her help and encouragement.

We worked together unceasingly. Ruth was indefatigable and optimistic and a constant inspiration. Her intellect, her integrity, her charm earned her many friends among parapsychologists.

I followed her advice and I always found her judgments to be wise and timely.

Ruth did indeed help me. There was nothing in my life I didn't share with her. She enabled me to give talks because I had no car. She drove me. She was my mentor.

One day she told me that another psychic friend had told her that we must go to Italy. Her information was that in the ruins of the ancient city of Herculaneum, buried only slightly below the surface, there lay a clay vessel. Sealed in the vessel were letters from the Apostle Paul. The letters would rival the Dead Sea Scrolls.

Her information was that I would pinpoint the vessel. "Do you think you could help?" asked Ruth.

It gave me chills to think about it. I had heard about psychic archeology. I was fascinated. "I don't know," I said. "I'll do what I can." I got in touch with an archeologist in Toronto who had experimented with this application of ESP. He was encouraging.

Ruth arranged reservations by air to Italy. Off we flew. We got into Rome the day before Easter. We had left so quickly we had no hotel bookings, as though we would have gotten a room anyway. We had no place to stay. I acted impulsively. I asked the driver of our car to stop at the next intersection. I got out. I approached the first person crossing the street. I told him in broken Italian which was mostly English that we had no place to sleep. He smiled obligingly and said to come with him. He beckoned to his wife. They got into our car and directed us to his house. He made a call, then they gave us keys. He took us next door to the apartment building and we entered an apartment. It was ours free of charge. It had marble floors and a view of the city. So now we had a place to stay. And then our host informed us that he was the chief of police in the coastal town of Ostia.

The next day, after we rushed out to the market to buy roses and wine which we presented to his family, we took the train to Naples. There we undertook our archeological reconnaissance mission with extrasensory perception.

In Naples we checked into a hotel. I sat on the bed with my automatic writing pad on my lap. I asked, "Where am I to go?"

After an interlude I wrote, "Go to Herculaneum and look for a garden lying between matching gates and arches. Behind them is a tree near the spot."

We set off wandering through the streets of Herculaneum. The mosaic beauty of the ruins was compelling. But we saw nothing to match my information. I couldn't find the twin arches.

I had no information to guide me further. But I kept walking. Then, suddenly, I felt I was being told exactly where to go. I climbed over a wooden barrier. "Come with me,"

I felt. "Come with me." I arrived onto a sidewalk and I turned around and there they were! The twin arches were there! "Ruth, look!" I said. And there between them was the gate.

"Where is the place?" asked Ruth.

"It's right here," I said, "but we can't touch it. We must have an archeologist find it and we will direct the archeologist."

I said to Ruth, "Is this madness? Is this possible?"

"This is not madness," said Ruth. "This is possible."

We photographed the site and the pictures with a written account of our psychic exploration were turned over to an archeologist who has previously used psychics to locate potential digs. Would a search in Herculaneum be successful? Do Paul's letters lie buried there? We do not have an answer. Only by daring to explore will we ever know. We may have been dealing with a fantasy. But always we remembered the story of the Lost Abbey in England, uncovered after centuries, and found by a psychic. A psychic who also happened to be an archeologist who dared to follow his intuitive clues.

Remembering Dreams
ESP and Children

As Shirley explained to me time and again during our many months of probing interviews, all of her ESP was not of murders and of lost bodies and lost airplanes. Neither was overmuch of her time devoted to convincing skeptics, however well-meaning, that she is, indeed, a true sensitive. If that were her fate as a sensitive, said Shirley, she would have regretted her powers.

Fortunately, Shirley enjoyed much of her ESP. Because of her association with Dr. Stanley Krippner who headed the famed "Dream Lab" at Maimonides Hospital, she became interested in dreams — precognition and telepathic dreams which were vividly accurate forerunners of actual events.

Sometimes, my children and I dream together. Here's an example. One morning, I called my daughter Maurine. I said, "I had a delightful dream last night. You were in it. I dreamed I walked down a lane toward a house surrounded by a white fence. I walked through a gate. The house had many windows and many panes in the windows. It had weathered shingles and lilac bushes on either side. I see it vividly. You were with me in the dream. We walked around the corner . . ."

"Wait a minute, mother," said Maurine. "I know what we saw. I had the same dream. I'll tell you the rest of it. Tell me if I'm right. Did we walk around the corner of the house and down a gently sloping lawn? Wasn't there a quietly flowing stream? Wasn't there a small, white boat tied to a pole? Did we get in the boat? Did I paddle you around?"

Yes. Yes. Yes.

"Then," I said, "we returned to the house to a lovely room with the sun coming in the window."

"Yes, mother," she said. "It gives me goose bumps to talk about it."

"Me too," I said. "It's our dream."

"Mother," said Maurine, "I feel we've been there."

"So do I," I said, "but I don't remember any such place. We only dreamed it. But we dreamed it together on the same night. It was a lovely experience. I felt as though I'd gone home to a very dear place."

"Me, too," said Maurine.

* * * *

All my life, I've had a recurring dream. It's always the same.

I am walking down a road lined with poplar trees. As I approach an intersection, I see a house. There is a long, open porch around it. The house is frame and surrounded by trees. It has a steeply pitched roof. The fields around the house are bare. I walk into the yard and people rush out to greet me.

In the dream I am crying and everybody coming to greet me is crying. It's as though I'd been gone for years and they are welcoming me back. These people are dear to me and I'm deeply happy to be home.

That is my recurring dream. I've dreamed it as a child, as a teenager, as a student and as a mother. In 1973, in April, I was driving south in Holland. We had just crossed the border into Belgium. I was with my second husband, Bill Cook. It was my first trip to Europe and I was very happy. What could be more exciting?

All of a sudden, we entered a countryside that caused my heart to pound so hard I went into an emotional state. I thought, what's happening to me? I was not sick. I looked through Lombardy Poplar lining the road. I looked across the fields. I began to recognize the landscape. Then, suddenly, I recognized the intersection ahead to be that of the road leading to "my" house. I was weeping uncontrollably. "Shirley?" Bill asked. "What's the matter? Do you want me to stop?"

"No," I said, "keep driving. Bill, it's the place of my dream. It's down there. If I go down that road, I will find my house and my people."

"Do you want me to take you there?" Bill asked.

"No," I said.

He drove on. As we passed the intersection and as it receded, I began to recover. I could breathe more easily. I returned to normal.

I have not had that dream again, but the memory of that place and those people stays clearly in my mind.

* * * *

Here is a dream that is also an out-of-body experience. It was in the spring of 1954. Mike, my husband, was graduating from college. We were living in a little apartment in Gorham, Maine.

In my dream the night was like black velvet. I could almost feel it. Suddenly I was looking down on a little town in Crystal, Maine. It was in the area of my home town of Island Falls. In fact, from the porch of my grandmother's house we could look over Crystal to Mount Katahdin. I recognized the town with delight.

In my dream, I saw Prescott's Potato Farm. I saw the railroad track and Frank Longstaff's house. And there, beyond a curve in the road, I saw two men walking. One of them was my father. He wore his fur hat and his laced khaki trousers tucked neatly into his boot packs. He wore his green plaid wool shirt. He carried his knife and knapsack. I thought to myself, "He has been trapping."

And then I saw a house billowing smoke. Then Father and his companion saw it. They rushed up the road and up the lane and onto the porch. They went into the house and soon had the porch stacked with sofas and furniture and books and lamps. There were clothes hanging on the line. They carried everything on the porch outside to the lawn.

Then I woke up. I was back in bed. I thought, "Isn't this peculiar? I know whose house that was." So, that next morning I wrote to my mother in Island Falls. I described the health of the children and Mike's coming graduation. At the end of the letter, I added: "You'd better alert our fire department because I dreamed a house in Crystal burned last night." And then I told her whose house it was.

A few days later I got mother's answer. It was not in her careful Spencerian script. She scrawled in letters nearly as high as the page. "Your house in Crystal burned last night! Your father discovered the fire! He tried to save their belongings, the house was locked. No one was at home. He saved everything that was on the porch."

* * * *

Here is a dream that my daughter, Margaret, recounted to me. Margaret is the director of a micro-biology laboratory in a large hospital.

"In my dream," said Margaret, "I was running down the street and I ran up to the door of a very large building. I opened the door, entered, and climbed a flight of stairs. In front of me on a hook hung a long red gown. I walked down a hall and opened another door. There lay my friend asleep. I woke her saying, 'You have to get up. We have to rescue her!'

"The two of us went downstairs and came upon a crumpled figure lying on the floor. It was an old woman. My friend and I carried her back to bed and tucked her in.

"The next day I went to work at the hospital. My friend was there. 'I have an interesting dream to tell you,' I said. 'It's so real I can't forget it.' I told her my dream.

"She looked at me in amazement. 'Margaret,' she said, 'last night I woke up as if someone had called me. I went down to the first floor. I found my aunt collapsed as if she had fallen while sleepwalking. It was very cold. I carried her back to bed. She was wearing a long, red, flannel nightie!'"

Was Margaret dreaming what her friend was, in fact, doing? I don't know. It is fascinating.

It would seem that when we sleep, the gate to the unconscious is open. Perception is unguarded and this freedom expresses itself in the telepathic and clairvoyant dream. What is more mysterious is the dream which reveals an event yet to happen.

When Margaret was in high school, she woke her sister Maurine one night with a strange and alarming statement. It was after midnight. Margaret was standing in front of the window looking out on the road. She was trembling.

"Maurine," she said. "There is going to be an auto accident!"

"Go back to sleep," said Maurine.

"It's going to happen right now!" said Margaret.

"You're dreaming," said Maurine. "Get back in bed."

"I can't!" said Margaret. "It's going to happen!"

At that instant a car roared past the window and crashed into the trees. It was someone we knew. The ambulance took him away and he lived. He had fallen asleep.

* * * *

In 1966 Mark, my son, was 16. The twins, only little fellows then, slept in bunk beds, double-decker. One night Mark still asleep, leaped out of bed and rushed into the twins' room. He caught Eric just as he fell out of the top bunk.

"When I woke up," said Mark, "Eric was in my arms."

Margaret Mead writes of a South Pacific culture in which dream telling is to the people what news watching and reading is to us. I feel I could live among those people. They might teach us a great deal.

* * * *

I feel a certain kind of telepathy has its origin in the close relationship between mother and child. And I feel it is usually the child who does the telepathy, not the mother. Young people can breathe easily because mother is not reading their mind. They are reading hers. Perhaps its nature's way of protecting children by giving them the advantages of telepathy.

In the time-tested story of Hansel and Gretel, the children are saved because they know their parents' intentions. I think children do, indeed, have that ability.

There are a number of instances I recall, but none so vivid in my memory as this one. We were living in what we called the little house. It was little all right. We had rebuilt a cottage far out in the country. We had no electricity and no plumbing. Not only was the cottage a dolls house, but we had sealed off the upstairs to conserve precious heat. We had a big cast iron kitchen stove which warmed our living room which was really quite attractive. In a portion of that room, Maurine had her crib on the other side of a partition. It was almost a room of her own.

She was not quite three and I had put her to bed in her crib. Maurine was saying nursery rhymes to herself out loud as she was in the habit of doing. She'd repeat them over and over until she got so sleepy her words trailed off. Then I knew she was asleep.

I opened the newspaper and read a gossip column by Dorothy Kilgallen. I stopped at a passage that read, "they lost their baby. Isn't it a shame because its death must have been a terrible tragedy."

I read with some emotion because I, too, had lost a baby. I found myself thinking it's a terrible thing. They lost their baby. It's a terrible thing.

Just then, Maurine, from her crib began to chant quite loudly in a sing-song refrain, "They've lost their baby. Oh, what a shame. They've lost their baby. Oh, what a shame..."

Maurine had picked up my thought in her sleep and repeated it.

* * * *

The most ordinary events in family life sometimes seem extraordinary to me. When my husband was going through college at the University of Maine at Gorham, our son Mark was a tiny baby.

On one occasion I remember vividly. I was getting ready for his 10 o'clock feeding. Maurine was in school. Margaret, our two-year-old, was in her tiny bedroom playing with her dolls and toys.

I was rummaging through the kitchen cabinet looking for the box of pabulum. I couldn't find it. I was thinking, where is the pabulum? What did I do with it?

Suddenly, from the bedroom Margaret called out loud and clear, "The baby's pabulum is all gone and you threw the box out, mother."

They were not the words of a two-year-old, but I knew Margaret had said them. I knew I hadn't spoken, not out loud. I went into the bedroom and asked Margaret, "How did you know what I was looking for? How did you know I was looking for the box of pabulum, Margaret? I didn't say anything, did I?"

"No," she said, once again in an adult manner, "you didn't say anything." She kept on playing busily.

"Well, Margaret, how did you know I wanted the pabulum? That I couldn't find it?"

Margaret looked puzzled, as if she couldn't think of a good answer. She continued to play with her dolls and toys. Then she said, "I saw it on your head."

*   *   *   *

My children have all shown some degree of ESP. The twins, Eric and Michael, demonstrated many times that telepathic communication between identical twins does indeed occur.

Eric, at about age two, proved his telepathic abilities also worked with his sister. She had been shopping in Portland for a surprise gift for her father. She came home late in the evening — long after the twins were asleep — and hid the package at the bottom of a pine blanket chest under stacks of sheets and pillowcases. The next morning, Eric came toddling through the hallway, lifted the lid of the blanket chest, dug the package out from the bottom and beaming happily gave it to his father saying, "Maurine wants you to have a present." The carefully kept secret was out.

*   *   *   *

George, too, showed he could do it when he chose. We were driving to the airport to meet the daughter of a friend whom we'd never met and someone said, "How are we going to recognize her?" George replied, "She will be dressed all in yellow with two yellow ribbons in her hair."

And she was.

*   *   *   *

When Michael, one of my twins, was three, I flew to New York to a parapsychology conference. A friend, Mrs. Hannaford, was taking care of my twins at her house. I told them I'd be gone three nights. I called them three "sleeps."

When I returned, Mrs. Hannaford told me this story. Two days after I left, Michael gathered up his toys and packed them in his suitcase. He hauled the case to the door and sat there. A plane came over and he called to Mrs. Hannaford, "Mommy is on that plane. She's coming back. She's coming to get me now."

"No," said Mrs. Hannaford. "Your mother won't come back until tomorrow. You have one more sleep."

"Oh, yes, she will," said Michael.

Two hours later, I was at the door. I had been on that airplane. I had come home a day ahead of schedule.

*   *   *   *

One afternoon in our house in West Buxton, we heard the wail of a siren and saw the fire truck go by. My husband Mike pulled on his coat and boots to help fight the fire. I looked out the window and down the road there was a bright, leaping glow behind the trees.

Michael was beside me on tiptoes peeking out the window. "The poor babies," he said, "all burned up."

"Oh no, Michael," I said. "It's probably just a fire that got into the woods."

"Poor babies," said Michael again, "all burned up."

I did not answer him.

Two hours later the fire was out and Mike drove into the yard. He came into the house looking desperate and exhausted. He was streaked with sweat and soot. His hair was singed, his hands blistered. He didn't notice them.

"Shirley," he said quietly, "both babies were trapped in their cribs. Both burned."

"I know, Mike," I said. "Michael told me."

I have observed that ESP is a natural phenomenon among children. We adults tend to have lost it.

*   *   *   *

Another incident of ESP involving my children, happened when Margaret was eleven. We wanted to get her a horse. We bought it from the owner of a mare about to foal. When it was born it was the most beautiful Palomino filly I have ever seen. At two months we brought it to our barn with the mother. Margaret began to take care of it.

Margaret did not weigh 75 pounds, but she did the grooming of both mother and filly. She cleaned the stall, carried bedding and water.

One day a man who knew horses came over to see how the three of them were getting along. He offered to break the filly when it was old enough. "You won't need to break this filly," said Margaret.

The filly had been raised with love. She never knew what unkindness was. We called her Misty, and Misty became one of our children. When she grew into a beautiful horse, we used to sit on the paddock fence with the twins. They were babies and their little pink toes dangled over the whitewashed boards. Misty would nuzzle their toes with her warm velvet lips and the twins would scream with glee.

Once the twins got into her paddock by accident. Misty froze, trembling, until we retrieved them. It was as if Misty were terrified she might step on the children who, of course, crawled toward her. When one of the babies was munching a cookie or a hot dog outside the paddock rail, Misty would would reach over and take it in her soft, gentle lips.

At seven months Margaret had trained Misty at voice command to come when called, to count her age in months with her hoof, to lie down, to bow and to run in circles.

Horse lovers came like tourists with movie cameras and Instamatics to document Misty's tricks. They couldn't believe an 11-year-old could teach Misty these tricks.

I tended to think that perhaps *only* a child could do it.

My ESP was keeping me preoccupied. The phone rang constantly and my mail came in canvas bags. I could respond to only a few letters a day, to only a few telephone calls. I was doing automatic writings for a caller when suddenly I got this message: "Watch your horse."

I asked why and I got, "Watch your horse. I can see her choking. When this happens act immediately or she will die." And then I got nothing more. I asked why, what? Nothing.

I resolved to watch Misty and to act promptly. It was winter and I worried expecting Misty to get pneumonia. After a week I let myself relax. I thought, oh well, it's just one of those things. I'm a worried mother of six and of a very smart horse.

One night I was busy putting the twins to bed when Margaret came rushing into the house. Her face was white. She said, "Daddy, Daddy, come quick. Misty is dying! Misty is dying! She is choking!" Margaret was panicked.

We rushed into the barn. Yes, Misty was choking.

I went to the phone and dialed Dr. Mackenzie in Saco. I said, "Doctor, get up here fast. Misty, our filly, is choking to death."

He knew the horse well. He had been our vet since we bought Misty. He must have driven like a state trooper because he was at the barn within minutes. It's eight miles. He worked on her and worked on her. A hay ball had lodged in her throat. She was, indeed, choking to death.

Then I remembered my automatic writing weeks before. "I see your horse choking. Act immediately or she will die. . ."

Medical ESP

Medical psychic perceptions fascinate Shirley, and some of her prognoses have proved stunningly accurate. She has earned the applause of audiences overwhelmed by her specific, descriptive pinpointing not only of the illness of the patient, but of his subsequent treatment.

Her diagnosis of Police Chief Frank Stevens during her role in the Olenchuk case is proved, as is her prognosis for Charles DeRoche, Sr., which is documented here in his letter of grateful thanks.

"I Charles DeRoche Sr. was a guest of Shirley Harrison one evening and she did a reading for me about my health. This was my first meeting with her and I was very surprised to learn she could know anything about myself or my physical health. She told me I was having a problem with my stomach and that I would need surgery, but that I would bounce back like a rubber ball.

"Two weeks prior to seeing Shirley I had been to see a doctor who only practiced internal medicine and he hoped to cure me with medicine. After seeing me he recommended my seeing a specialist at Maine Medical.

"At the time of seeing Shirley there had been no decision by the doctors on my stomach problem. It was a few days after seeing her, that the doctor told me the only way to cure my stomach problem was to have surgery. Shirley had been quite accurate in all she told me that evening, even to the fact that I would bounce right back like a rubber ball.

"I was and still am amazed at her prediction.

"I swear that this is a true and honest affidavit.

Charles A. DeRoche Sr."

Yet Shirley does not claim to be a psychic healer. In fact, she makes no claim at all other than warm, human, com-

*passion for those who may need her help. She warns that
medical psychic diagnosis is subject to all of the vagaries of
any other application of ESP. It is useful only in that it
explores another facet of psychic phenomena. It can also be
subject to an odd, psychic quirk called distortion as Shirley
explains here in the context of several experiences she relates
of medical ESP.*

Once I said to a person at an informal gathering of friends,
"You're going to have trouble with your gall bladder because
I see the scar." The person unhesitatingly pulled up his shirt
and there was the scar.

"I've already had the operation," he said.

That's an example of distortion in ESP. I'm not always
sure about time. I'm not sure whether an event is about to
happen or has already happened or is happening right this
instant.

Georgia Greely, who was to become vice president of the
National Association of Nursing Anaesthesiologists, introduced herself to me after a lecture at Westbrook College.

I said, "Georgia, you have an adrenal insufficiency. You
will have surgery soon to correct this."

"How did you know that?" asked Georgia.

I am no student of anatomy or of medicine. The words
came to me and I spoke them. She later had the operation I
described.

* * * *

Once I was a patient at the Bar Mills Hospital. I was suffering from anemia which has been my fate most of my life. The
doctor came in to see me.

"Mrs. Harrison," he quipped. "Let's see you do some ESP.
What about the patient downstairs?"

I said that first they must give him a haircut and then
they must take out his appendix. The nurses just howled and
so did the doctor. The new patient was a boy with hair over
his eyes. Sure enough, they took him to Portland and removed
his appendix.

* * * *

Another time, my daughter had a severe pain in her left shoulder. It was intense. I stood behind her and held my left hand an inch above her shoulder. After a brief while, less than a minute, she said, "Mother, don't burn me." When I took my hand away her skin was pink. And my hand tingled and it too felt warm. The pain in her shoulder had eased.

My friend, Thelma Moss has photographed such a hand and you can see an aura of energy radiating between the hand and the person's body. Her photograph of lovers kissing is like a neon sign. It's wonderful. The many examples of Kirlian photography show this.

* * * *

I was having tea with a woman I had just met at the home of a friend. I suddenly said, "You have a chipped bone in your ankle. It pains you."

"Yes, I do," she said. "How did you know that?"

I told her candidly that my attention had been drawn to that part of her leg and I sensed that it was "not right."

"I did it riding horseback," she said.

* * * *

Once I was scheduled to lecture for a Kiwanis club in the Portland area. I had a cold and I could feel laryngitis coming on. It was an effort to get there and I had difficulty speaking. As I looked around the head table I could see several critical faces. They said to me very clearly in their manner, we don't believe you can do these things we have heard about you.

I went on with my talk. Suddenly a man raised his hand. "I have a letter here," he said. "Could you tell us anything about the person who wrote this?" And he handed me the letter.

"I don't know," I said, "but I'll try. I might not be able to on this particular occasion."

I held the letter and I said that I could see the writer in the intensive care ward of the Maine Medical Center. "He's under 24-hour nursing. He's critically ill. He has had a coronary followed by pneumonia." And then I described the street where he lived, the houses on either side of his. There was a yellow house on one side and a gray house on the other. So I described them. Someone who knew the missing letter writer well exclaimed, "You're absolutely right."

The audience broke into applause. It was a rousingly successful evening. I could hardly get away from their eager questions.

Enigma of Distortion

We are skimming now. We can explore in depth as we go along. That will be our procedure. That's the way memory works. Questions generate new thoughts, memories, feelings. For example, I was thinking as I drove to work this morning that ESP does not distort reality. It adds another dimension. It's the sixth sense, of course. We are not limited to five senses. It's truly another sense. It's a natural part of us. Nevertheless, I have found a strange distortion in ESP and I attribute it to the conscious mind trying to evaluate ESP material. Here's an example.

Charles Honorton, a psychologist working at Maimonedes Dream Lab in Brooklyn with Stanley Krippner, asked me to do some ESP for him, casually, for fun.

I said, "Well Charles, why is it you have to go out of your office and down the hall just to answer the telephone?"

He burst out laughing. "Shirley," he said, "my personal secretary has an office next to mine. She takes all my calls and relays them to me. Her name is Miss Hall!"

That's distortion. My conscious mind confused the meaning of hall.

Here's another example of distortion.

I was working on a case in Freeport for the authorities. A five-year-old boy was missing and I had been asked by a lawyer to give my impressions of who had taken this child. I was doing automatic writing. I said, "If you round up all of the men out on probation from state prison who have been found guilty of a sex crime against a minor, and if you find the one living in Freeport, you'll have the criminal." Do you know, they did not do that. They were too skeptical. I continued to work on it. The name or the words Mill Town came to me over and over. I asked around: Was Freeport a mill town? I guess all those towns are mill towns, but I don't think Freeport is known as one. They finally got the guy. He was indeed, a sex offender out on parole. His name was Milton.

Another example of distortion, this time in a dream of my daughter, Margaret's.

Just before going to bed the other night, I got a telephone call from a young lawyer who was going to be renting an apartment in my house. We discussed his upcoming exam for the bar. He was studying very hard and he was anxious about his success. Eric, my son, and I were sitting in the living room eating artichokes. We dipped the leaves in homemade mayonnaise.

The next day Margaret came to take me to the beach and to have lunch. She said she'd had a strange dream the night before. She dreamed she was studying for the bar exam and at the same time eating artichokes and dipping the leaves in mayonnaise with curry sauce.

I loved it. I said, "You've done it again, Margaret." We both had a good laugh. We've done this before.

In the story of Margaret's dream about the elderly woman who fell during the night and was lying helpless on a cold corridor floor, Margaret dreamed that, as she climbed a flight of stairs to summon help for the stricken woman, she saw a long red gown hanging from a hook on the wall. In real life, when Margaret's friend found the frail old woman crumpled on the floor, she was wearing a long red flannel nightgown. There again, a slight distortion of reality.

In the case of the missing airplane, I initially told Mr. Bracy that the plane had gone down west of the town of Gossville. I had spent only about a half an hour on trying to zero in on it. When I concentrated on it for a longer time, I came up with the name Gosstown. I then checked it over several times against the first name "Gossville" finally choosing Gosstown as the correct location.

I don't think the information is wrong. The fault must lie in my interpretation.

A fact is a fact. If a man has run away to Georgia, he's run away to Georgia. If I'm trying to find him and I can't tune into that fact, then obviously I'm not able to make the connection. That baffles me. It baffles researchers in parapsychology. Is there a more profound reason? Am I not meant to know?

Here's another example. A man disappeared from a private hospital in Augusta. His parents called me. I got the impression he had hurt his head. He had fallen. He was badly injured. Well, they finally found him. He was alive. He had had a mental breakdown. I don't know yet if I was entirely accurate or if my information "hurt his head" was another example of my misinterpretation. The "hurt" in his head may have been my distorted impression of his mental illness. But that was all I could get on him. I couldn't get where he was or anything else about him. I felt my ESP was a failure. No, it doesn't always work.

It's tantalizing because of that. It's frustrating to want to use your ESP to help and then be unable to make it work. That's why I've never felt this is something I can take credit for. A good doctor can take credit for the control of his skill because he has spent many years preparing himself. Any person good at his work may take credit for that skill.

I do try. But the skill of it is not my skill. Do you understand? If I were in total control, I'd use ESP much more than I do.

Dr. Krippner has described ESP as coming from a voluntarily controlled altered conscious state. I agree. And to relax and get "into" that state of mind is difficult, and sometimes impossible to do.

The psychic, obviously, is in close touch with the unconscious — able to dip in and out of it easily. It is, however, impossible to do this consistently as so many variables affect the psi function. Stress, fatigue, depression — all negate it. It works best in an atmosphere of quiet relaxed receptivity. Such moments are hard to find in a hectic everyday schedule.

At its best, ESP is a fragile means of communication. The empathy between the psychic and the subject is tenuous. Distortion is a result of this fragility.

Testing Her Powers

Although Shirley lacked the academic training and title of a research scientist, she could, in fact, do what the scientists themselves were researching. Hers was the phenomenon. Hers was the mystery.

And so it was, time and again, from New England to North Carolina, and from Connecticut to California, Shirley was called to speak before conferences of scientists. It was at these conferences that dedicated professional parapsychologists rose to brief each other on the state of their research art.

Sometimes, in fact, it was Shirley who gave their keynote address. At the Menninger Foundation seminar in Kansas City, it was she who set the tone of the conference, and it was she who asked the primary questions foremost in the minds of all who would understand ESP.

"Could one human mind communicate with another via so-called sixth sense — a sense infinitely more sensitive than the first primitive five: seeing, hearing, feeling, tasting and touching?"

"Could a thought or image in one mind be sent directly to another mind and there be reproduced and recognized?"

"If this is possible," asked Shirley, "how can this power be developed and used? Is it a power we can control, or does it come to us intermittently like flashes of lightning? Is it a power we can originate ourselves and use regularly at will so that it becomes a sixth sense on which we can depend? Is it, in fact, a potentially normal means of human perception?"

These are some of the questions Shirley asked. She knew well that telepathy was real. She had experienced it herself. Yet, its source and mechanism remained a mystery to her. She knew it worked well across the room, and that it worked equally well over distances of thousands of miles. She knew also that it crossed the so-called barriers of time because she had communicated with minds she later learned were describing the future.

She reminded the scientists that beliefs in the immortality of the soul, in an astral body, and in spirits roaming among heavenly regions are closely linked with systems of thought as are found in most religions.

She pointed out that there are primitive animistic beliefs that it is possible to leave the body during sleep and to re-enter it upon awakening; and to leave it for good at the moment of death. She professed her personal belief in the immortality of the soul and in the uniqueness of the individual.

Shirley said also that physics does not forbid the transmission of intelligence from the future to the present. She emphasized that there was nothing supernatural, nothing, in fact, mysterious, about her ability to read thoughts.

ESP is a force related to people, she said. It is a force that can be directed by energy produced by our minds. We can register our brain waves on an EEG, she said, but we still don't have an instrument other than a human being that can register our thoughts.

Shirley urged the scientists to take ESP out of the dark ages of mysticism and find out how it works, because, she affirmed, it does work. She said she was surprised that scientists and artists, and, in fact, all creative people; all who strive to give meaning to the mystery of life, don't recognize that ESP happens often in their own lives.

In her lectures and talks delivered at scientific conferences, Shirley conceded that ESP may, indeed, be spontaneous. Yet, also she knew she had brought it within her control. In her work for parapsychologists, for police, for the FAA, she had been able to learn specific facts on demand about a prearranged subject.

Fearlessly, Shirley made her psychic visions public. She told intimate details that were not trifles about her ESP experiences, experiences she would not deny even if they seemed incredible. One such incident is especially revealing.

Shirley had been asked by her long-time liaison at the Federal Aviation Administration to find an aircraft reported missing. She had done this several times, of course, sometimes with astonishingly accurate results. This time, she said, her information about the missing plane was transmitted through a fisherman.

His name was Daniel Halsey, said Shirley. He told Shirley he grew up on Peak's Island in Maine's Casco Bay. He told Shirley that his mother bore a striking resemblance to Shirley and that "she would have taken a liking to you." He said he had been drowned in a winter storm about 30 years ago.

And then, Shirley said Daniel Halsey told her that an airplane which Shirley was attempting to locate had gone down in 120 feet of water at the channel buoy at the entrance to Hussey Sound. He said that it was in a shallow hole on the bottom and it was "easy to see." He said there were two men in the plane and they had a lot of money with them.

This information was as real to her as if she had heard a news account on the radio. In fact, she had passed on the information to the FAA. Her colleague there, said Shirley, reported back that, yes, computerized data based on wreckage found along the shore confirmed Shirley's (and Daniel Halsey's) information. He implied there may be insurance reasons for locating the wreck and the bodies in it. For those reasons, he said, a submarine would be hired and sent to the bottom of Hussey Sound. The submarine searched, but it did not find an airplane. The depth was 120 at Red Nun 4, he confirmed, right in the entrance to Hussey Sound.

At the same time, said Shirley, she was interviewed by a local weekly newspaper. She told this story: and the weekly printed it.

"I was willing to risk being wrong, even in public," she said. In an area where reputations are more easily lost than made, Shirley told what she knew. "ESP must be reported," she said. "It must come out of the closet, even at the risk of my credibility."

Consumed by curiosity, confident of her ESP, Shirley opened the telephone book to Halsey. There was, indeed, a listing. Its address was Peak's Island, Casco Bay. Could her source have been an ancestor? "I think that airplane is there," insisted Shirley.

Challenging? Yes. By Shirley's charismatic presence, golden-haired and clear-voiced, she reaffirmed that ESP was a power both passionate and humane. It was clear that she was one of the bold, bright, personalities who release the psychic radiant. Her eloquent address was one to rally the scientists. If anybody could banish misgivings about the new and obscure, she said, it was the scientists and their scientific proof.

She urged her colleagues to apply the most disciplined science to explore what she knew to be an intangible, even a metaphysical, power. She said that their statistical reports of carefully controlled experiments were critically important to ESP and that together they would expand the frontier of laboratory parapsychology.

Shirley's talks, of which she has retained her notes, were followed invariably by applause and accolades.

She was soon to organize her own conference on parapsychology It was the first in Northern New England and it was held at the University of Southern Maine at Gorham.

Her scientist peers repaid her in kind. They accepted her invitations to attend. Present were Gardner Murphy, famed successor to William James and Dr. Walter Franklin Prince, as the third American to be president of the Society for Psychical Research. Murphy was also Director of Research at the highly esteemed Menninger Foundation in Topeka, Kansas, and he had been president of the American Psychological Association in 1944. He had edited a collection of essays entitled *William James on Psychical Research* and he had held a Richard Hodgson Fellowship at Harvard.

Also at Shirley's conference were: Dr. William Wolfson of Detroit; Dr. Jule Eisenbud, University of Colorado Medical School; Dr. Bernard Grad, McGill University; Charles Honorton and Dr. Montague Ullman, Maimonides Medical Center, Brooklyn, N. Y.; Sister Justa Smith, Rosary Hill College, Buffalo, N. Y.; Dr. Stanley Krippner, Humanistic Psychology Association, San Francisco, California; Dr. Thelma Moss, Department of Psychology, U.C.L.A.; Douglas Dean, Newark College of Engineering, and many others.

The event and the place held much personal meaning for Shirley. It was here that her husband attended college and was graduated. Shirley had worked with him, tutoring and typing and had herself planned to finish her education at this college.

Now Shirley's conference at the university was reported

nationally in the journals of parapsychology. It proved to be a success. Not only that, at long last it seemed to celebrate the fact that a true sensitive herself was directing a public seminar of research in parapsychology. For Shirley, this was a breakthrough.

Shirley recalls that the scientists read their papers. "They reported," she said, "on the probability factors above chance that proved that psi was operating." They had done their research with cards and there was little feeling in their long and detailed reports.

Yet they were necessary. What ESP needed most of all in the modern world was scientific explanation. On this the scientists were in accord. Shirley herself had been a subject of their research.

In 1963 several years before the conference at the University of Southern Maine, Dr. Louisa E. Rhine, that most eminent pioneer of parapsychology, introduced Shirley to William Roll project director of the Psychical Research Foundation at Duke University in Durham, North Carolina. The Rhines (Louisa's husband, J. B. Rhine, was equally involved in ESP research) had defined the modern-day domain of parapsychology and made it a household word. At work at Duke, they emphasized the importance of rigorous controls, quantitative results, and statistical analysis.

They proved conclusively to the nation that ESP was based in fact. Fundamental to the Rhines was objectivism. They, the scientists, would stand aside. They would be observers, neutral and emotionally uninvolved.

William Roll was intrigued by the opportunity to conduct carefully controlled tests of Shirley Harrison's ESP powers. He extended an invitation to her to spend time in Durham and be the subject of extensive testing and research into the mysteries of ESP and of her own powers.

Shirley was delighted by William Roll's invitation and accepted it. She had always believed that her ESP acted in accord with natural laws. Only what were the laws? Now, perhaps, she would find out. Part of the answer surprised Shirley and the scientists themselves.

William G. Roll is a modest, diligent scientist who would discover ESP by the effect it produces. He was determined to prove to the satisfaction of his colleagues that what he had observed had actually occurred and would occur again under similar circumstances. One of his specialties, about which he held theories he wished to prove, was psychometry.

Although psychic sensitives vary tremendously in their specialties, nearly all of them have in common the practice of psychometry: getting psychic impressions about a person or object by holding an object belonging to him or to her, or by holding the object itself. Shirley had baffled and astounded audiences by feats of psychometry. On television, she had held a piece of wire and told many thousands of viewers that it was "a piece of the Berlin Wall." It was.

Countless times before an audience Shirley had described the professions and living rooms of owners of such mundane objects as pens and pencils.

Now, Roll personally asked to work with Shirley. One of Roll's theories described in reference works on parapsychology utilized the concept of a psychic field (psi) which he likened to electromagnetic or gravitational fields. Every object, living or non-living, he theorized, has a psychic field. In the case of ESP, a psychic or mental event at the target or source produces a psychic trace which is then communicated to the psychic field of the sensitive. It interacts with the sensitive's brain and the brain's mental bank to produce ESP.

In telepathy, Roll theorized, a sensitive's memory produces information that resembles the psychic trace of the target. It is this information that emerges into consciousness and that serves as evidence for telepathy.

Contrary to Shirley's first expectations, they worked not in a sterile laboratory, but in Bill Roll's dining room where they could look out on a garden.

"There was a fig tree bearing ripe fruit," Shirley remembers. "There were flowers everywhere and there were song birds serenading and darting about in the trees around the house."

In that atmosphere of serenity, they spent three days testing, from October 9-12, 1963. Long and tiring as the tests were, Shirley took them easily. In comparison to earlier psychic chores, it was far more rewarding to take these tests than to recreate by way of example the intensity and authenticity of ESP before an audience of solemn-minded nay-sayers.

That had often been a painfully hard task, yet she had performed it many times.

What had she to gain from public demonstrations of her gift? She was put to a deal of trouble. She did what she was asked to do. She got results. Sometimes, called in the night over the telephone, she did her best and then heard no more about it. Perhaps she had helped a few people. Or perhaps, even if she did all that was asked of her, her questioners remained unconvinced.

Compared to her public performances as a sensitive, scientific testing was entirely worthwhile.

Shirley suffered no embarrassment by being asked to compete against scientific controls. On the contrary, she acted as if it were the most natural thing in the world. The surroundings suited her. The manner of the experimenting scientist was deferential.

"To me," said Shirley, "the tests with Bill Roll were well organized. I sat at a table. In front of me, stapled to a white piece of cardboard, were four sealed envelopes.

"Bill handed me four similar envelopes. They, too, were sealed. My job was to match these four with the four on the table. I was to match them in pairs as I felt they should go."

For days, Shirley matched envelopes as Bill Roll handed them to her. They worked for hour after hour, set after set.

"I would not admit to being tired," said Shirley. "I felt the tests were terribly important, and I knew that I had the ability to just 'know things' about the envelopes!"

Both Roll and Shirley, too, were curious to learn the results of these preliminary tests. Less than three months later, on December 2, 1963, Roll wrote Shirley the news they all hoped most for.

His letter reveals the importance he placed on his work with her.

"We got some excellent results from our tests!" he exulted. "I reported on them to my colleagues at Duke and they were very excited. The matching experiments in which you were able to match pairs of cards only on the basis of their association in the past with certain persons represents a breakthrough in scientific testing in this area. These pairs of cards were identical and indistinguishable from each other, except that some of them had been in contact with specific persons.

You appeared to be able to sense some 'psychical' emanation from them and so tell which two cards *originally belonged together*. We must pursue this further! Are you willing to go ahead?"

Shirley was willing, indeed! This was a chance to support her personal faith with the knowledge and wisdom of empirical inquiry. She knew that, at times, she had the special endowment to achieve ESP. She felt that with special training in the art of mental concentration, perhaps ESP could be cultivated and used deliberately, just as in any other object of study such as chemistry or physics.

She also felt an exhilarating sense of worthwhileness in pursuing problems of cosmic dimensions. This was a feeling she shared with William James himself, with Dr. Montague Ullman, with her mentor, Ruth Hyde, and with many others.

Spontaneity and genuine freedom, she felt, would be hers, if only she could continue her ESP. However, psychic sensitives, themselves bold and bright and able to actually do what the scientists can only observe, are subject to peaks and valleys in their powers. It is the price Shirley paid, she knew, for her clairvoyance. Despite these vicissitudes, help was continually requested and she cheerfully gave it. She solved many perplexing and difficult cases. She had performed on cue and under terrific pressures. She was able to assume a quiet, relaxed state of mind and to tap her powers even under police escort, in blizzards, in airplanes and while calming distraught parents and relatives.

At times, her ability deserted her only to reappear when she could relax and with extraordinary concentration, will herself that inner quiet and peace that would unblock the flow of her ESP. There would be troubled periods in her life when she was beset by personal anxieties. "At those times," said Shirley, "my powers lay hidden. I was unable to draw on them." Yet, they returned again and again. She learned to wait for them.

The relationship between religion and psychical research in Shirley's attitude is a clear one. Mental healing, also, was of deep interest to her. All of them were important, even cosmic manifestations of little-understood areas of the human mind and its powers. Hers was a metaphysical inquiry that made the richest possible contact with the concrete, the immediate, the real.

Yes, she answered Bill Roll, she was willing to go ahead.

Then Bill Roll, on behalf of his colleagues nationally and at the Psychical Research Foundation, welcomed Shirley to their group. Here was the culmination she had dreamed of ever since her first days of ESP awareness in Island Falls with Dr. Swett.

Bill Roll was to test Shirley again, as his published report of his research reveals. This time he travelled to Saco, Maine, for further explorations with Shirley to develop his theories. He proved to be a meticulous craftsman in his science. He prepared his experiments thoroughly and documented each step in their preparation. He sealed his packages of cards so that not even air, which may indeed possess a psychic trace, could reach them.

In addition, he tested the psychological stability and creative potential of his sensitives. He gave them Rorschach personality tests. He would measure their minds in many ways, thus exploring, for example, a possible relationship between ESP ability and creativity. Indeed, Shirley's Rorschach resumé mentioned her creative ability.

Other sensitives tested by Roll were found to be undergoing considerable emotional turmoil underneath a quiet exterior, but that was not the case with Shirley Harrison.

These second tests duplicated the first. They too, were successful and above the level of chance. His description of these tests as he published them in the Journal of the American Society for Psychical Research, Volume 60, October, 1966, Number 4, may be of interest to those who wish to pursue the subject further and in greater depth.

At the conclusion of Bill Roll's testing with Shirley, he felt important strides had been made in the investigation of psychic abilities.

Dispelling the Myths

As Shirley's fame broadened, she learned that there were many myths about ESP in the public mind, myths she would strive to debunk. In these parts of Shirley's story in her own words, she exposes several inaccurate yet popular notions about ESP. Here she discounts the misconception that psychics are able to use their powers of precognition to guide them safely and easily through life, perhaps even to make themselves rich by predicting the vagaries of the stock market or the winners at the track. If this is not possible, some ask, what good is ESP?

Yet, Shirley has, indeed, used her powers of precognition for useful purposes. She has saved lives, other people's lives, lives of people whom she loved.

In addition, we learn here that Shirley, the renowned sensitive, is sometimes asked for advice requiring not so much the knowledge of a psychic, but of a loving mother and a wise and compassionate person. In fact, in this case Shirley offered practical wisdom that her questioner may have known already to be true.

Many people think of ESP in only one way: predicting the future. That is only a small part of psychic sensitivity, although it is an important part.

In any case, why do we want to know what lies ahead? Why is that important? I don't seek it. There have been times when it worked for me, times when I was given information to help somebody I loved. But to help me personally? Nothing. It cannot. I stumble and fall and get scraped and suffer and make bad decisions.

I have heard people say, "Oh, you live a charmed life. Oh, you know everything." Nonsense. The psychic person is not omnipotent. We see as through a glass darkly. And sometimes we see by surprise.

Precognition, for example, seems to happen spontaneously. It has slipped in sideways while I was trying to do something else, prepare dinner, say, or vacuum the living room rug.

I have never been able to sit down on Monday morning and say today I will predict and then rattle off oracular remarks about Farah Fawcett or Elizabeth Taylor or airplane crashes and earthquakes and assassinations and wars. Anybody can do that because the law of averages will guarantee their success.

True precognition is elusive, yet it can be specific. Place and details can be astonishingly clear. And if it is about a person it can be so detailed that it can apply to that person only.

Unfortunately, there is a style of psychic showbusiness that tells people they are going on trips and are coming into some money and are crossing water and are going to have a lover. This damages the integrity of parapsychology and erodes the credibility of the true psychic reseacher.

In cases of true precognition, I don't frighten and intimidate. I use only what I have learned which I think will be helpful. I am discreet. I don't think precognitive knowledge should be used if it is negative and potentially destructive. In any case, seldom do I get ominous information. I do not seek it.

But sometimes it does indeed happen that way. I was once asked by a nurse about a patient. Suddenly I said, "I know he will die on Friday," and I gave the date. And he did. I am not interested in that kind of information. It's not useful. I don't want to know how long others are going to live, or for that matter how long I am going to live. Yet, occasionally this information comes through.

The personality of a sensitive is open and childlike. It is unguarded and trusting. I remember my mother saying that she didn't think I had reached the age of reason until I was 30, and then she had doubts. She was right. I still love, at times, to actually be a child again.

I remember an incident when my twins were four and playing hide and seek and hiding in the blanket chest. I joined them. I hid in the blanket chest, too, and sprang out of it yelling Boo! Eric cried. I realized that I was being a child a little too hard. But it was such great fun. They loved the games we played.

I feel we must approach learning with the open-minded, unguarded curiosity of a child. Only that way can we discover new knowledge.

Many of my spontaneous ESP experiences are related to my children. When my daughter, Maurine, graduated from college, she went to work as a dental hygienest. She got her own apartment in a city about 40 miles from our home. One morning I was baking bread and it occurred to me with urgent clarity that Maurine must have health insurance and she must have it now! I called her.

"Not now, mother," she said. "Later."

"Not later," I insisted. "Now. In fact, I will drive over with the check."

"ESP again, I suppose?" Maurine said, laughingly.

I insisted. I called her again the next day. This time Maurine called her insurance agent. He drove over and they signed the policy. Four days later, Maurine was rushed to Mercy hospital. She had acute appendicitis. The insurance agent protested. He questioned the claim. He was convinced we had prior knowledge.

The doctor certified that it was an acute attack and that she had no history of chronic appendicitis. The company paid the bill. My ESP proved itself once again in the practical world.

Another example of truly compassionate precognitive ESP concerns a child I had never seen. This time, once again, my ESP was specific and I feel I had foreknowledge of what was in store for the child at the hands of his parents. I felt the child was in danger. This incident occurred when I was telephoned by an anxious lady. I sensed her wisdom and humanity over the telephone. She asked me to try to help her family, that there was a boy in great trouble.

I felt I should try to help, but I also put her off a day and then a week. I had to wait. And then, after several weeks, I was doing automatic writing, as the researchers with whom I was co-operating had asked that I use the ability in as many ways as possible and to keep records.

Suddenly these words came:

"Five entities will speak. The first will speak to the boy's mother. The second will speak to the boy's father. The third will speak to the boy's grandmother. The fourth will speak to the boy's grandfather. The fifth will speak to the boy himself."

And then, each in turn, they began to write with my hand on my pad of paper. The first entity said to the mother: "Where is the heart's love you should give this child? Where is the mother's love? You view him coldly. You do not see beneath the surface of his life. You do not try to understand how he feels. You were given this precious gift of life and you have rejected the gift. Consider what you are doing. Ask yourself why you are doing this."

The second entity said to the father: "I chide you for not spending your time with your son, for placing your own ambitions above your love for the boy, for treating the child not with love, but with criticism; cold, calculating criticism. It is based in ambition and pride. You must love this child for what he is; not what you expect him to be."

The third entity said to the grandmother who loved the child: "This is what you can do for the boy. See to it he does not have to leave the place he loves. See to it he can live outdoors until he grows in wisdom. Do not send him away among strangers to be educated. That is not what he needs."

The fourth entity said to the grandfather: "You can fill a great need in this boy by giving him your time. Tell him about your life when you were a boy, for you were very like him. Tell him about his family. Give him renewed pride in himself."

And the fifth entity spoke to the boy himself: "You are a human being, precious and unique. Whatever happens to you in your life, remember you are an important person."

I relayed this information to the grandmother. She wrote to me saying that I had perceived the situation accurately. She followed the advice I had given her. She felt it was a God-given message to her.

Admittedly ESP is inconsistent. Yet when it occurs it is astounding. Admittedly, also, I am the medium of this knowledge and I am a person with all the human feelings.

It annoys me when people scoff and say, "Oh, well, yes, she was right on this one, but she was wrong on that one." What do they expect me to be. I am an ordinary person. I am a mother and a working woman. I resent the feeling that because I have a kind of psychic sensitivity, I am a cross between Joan of Arc and Tinkerbell.

The bigots associate me with white witchery and powdery incantations and spells. Ridiculous nonsense! The only magic is in the marvelous potential of the human mind and spirit. It's not in amulets and rituals. If I could wear an amulet that would ward off all misfortune and solve all of my problems, I would be the first person to buy such an amulet. The real world is not that way. There is no magic.

If you want to understand psychic sensitivity as I do, do not discredit a sensitive for making a mistake. Do you expect a doctor to make a correct diagnosis every time? The best doctors constantly question their knowledge. That is how they learn. And a psychic does not have the information that is provided to a doctor. A psychic has nothing but strong intuitive feelings.

The cynics expect absolute perfection, and if they don't get it they say I told you so.

The student of ESP, the parapsychologist, realizes the absurity of that kind of thinking because it's a wonder that ESP works at all. The people who say ESP is hogwash and hocuspocus will go to extremes to explain it away. They get irrational about it. They can't accept anything for which there is no present explanation, forgetting that we are limited by the scope of our present textbook knowledge.

Another annoyance is the pulp writer's predilection for distorting ESP into something evil. They make it frightening. They make it obscene. Children are born with extrasensory perception or expanded awareness. It has nothing to do with our concept of the devil, but is rather a poorly understood potential of the mind.

I resent pulp writers and film makers who clothe ESP in mystical, black, bloody garments. ESP is an intuitive way of learning. Why should that frighten us? Are we back in the days of the Salem witch trials? Shouldn't we leave that behind us? Are we still those people who relegate to the dark supernatural everything they don't understand?

Parapsychologists accept ESP as part of the natural workings of the mind and study it as such.

I have been challenged by fundamentalists who raged that ESP is a voice of the devil and that these are evil spirits. I would like one of them to show me anything evil that ever came out of ESP. The fact is that everything I have ever seen come out of it is prompted by love, by caring, by helping, by a desire to know. If they say this is the devil's way, they speak nonsense.

A fundamentalist minister accosted me just bristling. He said that God had spoken to him many times, constantly, in fact, spoke to him and guided him. I listened to my challenger and I thought him truthful. I did not doubt him.

And then I asked whether he felt himself to be unique? To be singled out from among us because of his experience as a minister? Would he concede that other people have these experiences?

It was plain to see in his manner that he considered himself unique. That when he had an ESP experience or a mystical experience, that God spoke to him. That when others had such an experience it was the devil's work.

Fairground psychics claim that they can "read" cards. Well, the cards are nothing, just pieces of paper. The information is coming through the mind. But they feel they have to explain their craft. So they use cards with pictures on them. The ancient lore about crystal balls and Ouija boards is merely an attempt to explain the telepathic function. Psychologists define it as a communication of the unconscious.

I am careful to explain to those questioning the reality of my ESP that all of the cases I have recorded, and in fact everything psychic I have ever done, can be traced to a real event. I mean by that, to something that has happened or is about to happen, in the real world. It is not something that I dragged up out of my emotional history and played out in fantasy.

If I had learned, after years of practicing parapsychology, that it was all imagination, all wishful thinking, I would have given it up years ago. My life has been so full. I have so many other interests that I would not have wasted my time in pursuit of an illusion. I would have been bored had it not been productive of factual information.

ESP is also very demanding of me. At the end of a session of concentration I am happy, but I am sometimes exhausted if

I stay with it too long, for too many hours. I have been told at such times that I am pale, ashen. ESP requires intense mental concentration.

Two doctors at a parapsychology conference once monitored me during ESP concentration. They reported that my pulse rate slowed ten points from the normal and was deep and steady. They reported that my eyes dilated. They said, "Shirley, you are in the Alpha State."

I thought to myself that I must also have been in the Alpha State while stirring the soup on the stove and watching two babies playing on the floor. Because I have learned, as a mother of six beautiful children, that if family life is peaceful there can be all kinds of rumpusing around me and it won't interfere with my concentration. I have learned to be innerly composed.

I liken the Alpha State to that of a jazz musician composing and playing for a noisy, happy, crowd. My ESP, like my music, is another form of creativity. Yet it is mysterious.

Good scientists acknowledge that we study the mystery. We don't study what we already know. Einstein said that to him that was the beauty of science.

But the scoffers in the scientific world say that if everybody can't do ESP and if it can't be done in a repeatable lab experiment, then forget it. In my mind those narrow-minded scientists ignore the fact that ESP does sometimes work, and when it works it is startling. I don't deny that ESP is inconsistent. Ironically, inconsistency is one of the marks of a true sensitive. The charlatans seem to be able to produce wonders on demand. I feel the scientists should study the mercurial nature of the psychic phenomenon. We should study the anomaly. Therein lies fresh knowledge.

The evidence for ESP precedes our knowledge of it. Unless we study the evidence, how are we ever going to develop the knowledge? It is only the fakes who are never wrong. It is only the fakes who are "right" all the time. Sometimes I write in my journal, "I couldn't do it today." Then, two days later: "Wow! What a day!"

Why is that?

I want my psychic sensitivity to remain pure. I don't want it tarnished with crassness. I'm wary of any distortion of

ESP to make it more exciting. It's already exciting. I don't want to elaborate just to impress or astound anybody.

When I give a talk, I am confronted with an audience that is waiting to hear mysterious, wonderful, things. What a temptation to embroider and become a storyteller. But I don't.

I believe that if we embellish our true account of ESP, we tarnish it and spoil it, and then we would be forced onto the defensive because we did not tell it just exactly the way it was.

Psychics over the ages seem to have been tested and exposed as people trapped them. I feel those psychics were driven by the need to comply and to please. People have tried to trap me. I refuse to be trapped. I will not compromise.

Yet, I actually enjoy a challenge. And if I can't do it, I say so: "I'm sorry, I can't do that."

The satisfaction of successfully demonstrating ESP is the reward for patience and persistence.

When I am confronted by people who are a blank, about whom I sense no information, I am baffled. I have learned these are sometimes depressed people, armored people. I've drawn that conclusion by observing them. There is a coldness about them. They are unforgiving and ungiving. They don't want to be part of warm, human life. The women of that type are not warm and the men of that type frighten me. It is because they do not have the human qualities of compassion and love, although they may have intellect.

A ruthless intellect is frightening to me and such people repel me. I automatically back away from them. They are powerful, perhaps supremely intelligent, but cold and unfeeling.

On the other hand, when you have a great intellect and with it a highly evolved humanity, then you have compassion and caring for people. That's when you have a human being worthy of the name. These are the Dr. Schweitzer's of the world. I sense their being. I feel it.

Spontaneous ESP is almost invariably fostered by concern for a loved one. It seems sometimes to be a reaching out in love.

There have been times when a feeling of love and affection filled a room of people and the ESP just came alive. It was thrilling.

There is a relationship between psychic sensitivity and the feeling of love, of loving and of being loved. A real caring of others is the heart and the soul of true religion. I cannot accept a religion or a doctrine based on fear and vengeance and intolerance.

Sometimes my questioners suggest that ESP is folklore. My answer is that in the sense that folklore implies story-telling based on myth, ESP is not folklore. But in the sense that folklore is the history of the knowledge of the people, then ESP is the purest form of it.

Jesus said it very clearly: ". . . even as I have done, you shall do also . . . and your young shall dream dreams."

I am convinced that Jesus demonstrated the ultimate in psychic sensitivity. He was the epitome of the perfect person. We cannot approach his divinity.

I don't think the psychic sensitive is a chosen person. The psychic is human with human foibles. I think it's presumptuous for a psychic to expect to be admired for "holy" qualities.

I suspect that true sensitives have developed ESP they had as children.

I've always enjoyed using my ESP in as many ways possible, in order to understand it, and myself, more fully.

I welcomed my lecture engagements for that reason. If I proved entertaining, good; but I was also learning things about myself which amazed me. And I think learning itself is a high form of entertainment.

I also think that a room full of people is conducive to ESP. There is an energy in the room. It has occurred to me that when Jesus referred to "two or more gathered in my name," he may have anticipated that communal energy.

Often I have been asked, can ESP be used for evil? The answer is that anything can be used for evil. There are ministers who should not be in the pulpit, doctors not fit to practice medicine, teachers who should not be teaching, psychic sensitives who claim a gift they do not hold to be sacred.

It's how we use ESP that makes it good or bad.

All the psychics I know personally are very fine people. I feel these sensitives empathize deeply with others and have deep insight into people's problems. They are gentle.

I also think that ESP develops a person's sense of inquiry. It helps that person shed armor; I mean the psychological armor we bind on to protect us from new ideas: In that way ESP is good.

I always want to look at people when I answer their questions or in doing telepathy experiments, as I do quite often before psychology students. It may make them uncomfortable, but I simply need eye contact with them. I don't know why. I try to put people at ease by explaining this and they usually relax and enjoy the experience.

It's not unusual for me to get a name as these cases will show. There are dozens of small incidents, many of them funny, harmless, practical jokes of ESP. Once at the Bethel Inn in north-central Maine, I gave a talk for women in banking. It was a hot day in summer and it was lunch time. I gave my talk and we had questions and answers. Afterwards, I went out in the lobby to cool off and relax.

Two women in the audience rushed up to me absolutely fascinated. I knew what they wanted, a personal example of ESP, something for them only. "What can you tell us?" they asked. "One little thing?"

It was so hot. All I wanted to do was get out of there. So I looked at one woman and said, "What does the name Jane Smith mean to you?"

"That's me," she shrieked.

Another time, I was speaking to a woman's club assembled in a living room. In the course of the evening the husband of their hostess came home. The club was busy with its meeting.

"Hello girls," said the husband sauntering into the hall. He leaned against the wall with one hand the way many men do. There was a sort of amused grin on his face. "Having a good time?" he said. "Well, Mrs. Harrison, what can you tell me about myself?"

This was the kind of challenge I love. It was humorous and I wondered if I might not be able to stun him into a more respectful attitude.

"What's wrong with your knee?" I asked. "You had an operation on it." And then I asked, "What does the name Dubois mean to you?"

He was stunned all right. He turned around. DUBOIS was printed on the back of his sweatshirt! And then he admitted he had had a knee operation. Those moments are a light-hearted upmanship.

Other cases are not at all lighthearted. They are tense, critical, cases in which the life of a child may be threatened. The parents, of course, are distraught or trying hard not to be.

The first missing person case I ever worked on involved a friend of mine, a book publisher in New York. She had a daughter who was distressing her. The child was going through the turbulent teens. She had run away.

The mother called me. I directed her to a corner which I named in New York. I said the building has a store on the first floor and an apartment upstairs. "Post a man at the front of the building and a man at the back and you will get her." They got the girl as she came out. She was with two men. I had even described accurately, so the mother confirmed, the dress the girl was wearing, the pocketbook she was carrying, and how much money she had.

A few days later a lovely silver dish arrived at my door and with it a note, "Thank you."

I still use it.

I am asked, do I have visions. My answer is, only in dreams. Dreams are a kind of vision. My ESP is verbal and it springs into my mind as a complete thought. Sometimes I do not know it until I have said it. Here is an example. One day I was having lunch with my friend, Jerry. And suddenly I asked him, "Who was the Red Fox?"

"Oh," he said, greatly surprised. "Where did you get that name? That was the code name for the leader of the IRA with whom my father served during the troubles."

Jerry explained that he was born in Ireland and that his father served with the Irish Republican Army.

I have to sit and wait for what I call the impression. Sometimes I wait twenty minutes, many hours. Yet sometimes I know instantly. To reaffirm the impression I ask again and wait for an answer, a confirming impression. If it comes to me as if it were a ping-ping on a radar scope and I get the feeling that I am right, then I am satisfied.

It is like looking for the missing piece of a puzzle. Yet the knowledge is not a vision. It is feeling — sensing. It is pure knowledge that I am right. It is what I call the Eureka Syndrome.

I have said several times that I suspect Jesus Christ was a psychic sensitive. He did it all. He demonstrated precognition. He did telepathy. He knew what those around him were thinking. He healed a woman. He did psychokinesis. He altered matter. He converted water into wine. He raised men from the dead. He was precocious as a child. In fact, he astounded people whom we would call trained observers today and he did that as a child.

Here is an incident that illustrated the way a sensitive child may learn about society and about the true plight of those around her. It happened to me.

I was ten. I was visiting my Danish grandmother, Karen Johnson in South Portland, Maine. We were Christmas shopping — which today I feel is a travesty of Christmas. This time I saw an old woman gazing into a shop. I looked into her eyes. I knew exactly what was in her mind. She did not have enough money to buy presents for her loved ones. I knew that with utter certainty. That knowledge doubled me over in anguish. I had learned that there was social injustice around me and that I could feel another's pain.

During my life, I have elected to accept the challenge of ESP. I feel it is opening a new area of the mind — or a very old area of the mind. It asks questions. Is this evidence of human immortality? Is this the voice of the soul? Is this proof of survival? I want to know.

Or is this mere wish fulfillment? Am I pleading, please tell me what I want to hear? At times I have felt that this life is all there is. There is nothing more. And then I have learned anew one inescapable fact. There is more. The fact is that again and again I learn information that cannot come from the unconscious mind because the source is beyond that. And what is the source?

I hope some day I will have absolute proof that truly there is life after death, that consciousness can exist without matter, that energy lives on and on, that intelligence survives!

It is still a viable question, one which neither science nor religion has answered beyond all doubt.

The complete skeptic about survival after death is probably the psychologist who is not a spiritist and who does not believe in survival. That person may, however, concede to the evidence of the power of telepathy. But that person might not concede that I have communicated with people who have died, as we call that state of life outside the body. But the evidence I have collected over twenty years proves to me that I have.

Parapsychologists need many more years of intense and careful research before this theory can be substantiated.

The materialists say that divorced from the body there is nothing. But I say there is the spirit. There is a surviving intelligence. And I say that is the next great mystery to be explored by science. That is the mystery Einstein and Freud wanted to explore. That is what William James wanted to explore. That is what parapsychologists are exploring. That is what I want most to explore.

One of the problems in doing ESP is that I can't always be objective because my own feelings creep in. That is true of doing ESP in any form, telepathy, psychometry, automatic writing.

That is why when I am asked to work on a case, I do not want to be told very much at all about it. Just give me the problem. No background. No descriptions. A name and a date will do. Otherwise my conscious mind will color in the outline I create out of the description. It is difficult to focus in, so to speak, with interference from my own emotions creating distractions. And I can't deny my emotions because they are much of what makes me Shirley Harrison. To do accurate ESP, I have to keep myself out of it and that's not always possible.

Some mild stimulants seem to help. A half cup of coffee is good for ESP. Alcohol is a depressant and would have a negative effect. Mind-altering drugs are abhorrent to me, and I deplore their use. Efforts to expand the mind by their use I term a short cut to Nirvana — a short cut which can end in disaster. But the worst enemies of ESP are the negative attitudes of armored cynicism. Just as that is the worst enemy of science.

Fatigue and stress seem to be negative factors. I find a positive attitude seems to dispel fatigue. I have found that boredom and anxiety are very negative states of mind, indeed, and they are terrible enemies of ESP. You must learn to be calm in the face of anxiety. Fear and hatred stifle ESP.

I cannot imagine a lethargic person doing ESP. It is for what we call "high energy" people. Such people learn calmness and it is the calmness of self-control.

And then, all the good things make it work better: good humor, pleasure, friendship, love, curiosity, and a good mixture of people in a room. That seems to develop something extra, something very positive and encouraging.

I do my best ESP when I am happiest.

I am frequently challenged in the matter of money. It seems much on the minds of those who inquire about ESP. I know of no other service to society which is not paid for. Doctors, priests, all are paid. Psychics must not be paid, some say. Why? If psychics should not be paid, then priests should not be paid. Although I have never demanded a fee, I have been told that if a sensitive demands a fee, the public recoils in horror. She is considered to be commercializing her gift. What a terrible crime!

They forget that the psychic has a skill which is valuable and that she, too, has to make her way in the world. Ironically, only if you give your psychic time freely does the public feel you are using your gift as God meant you to, to help others. I have lived with this for many years. I am paid to entertain people by lecturing and I have given lectures by the dozen. But to help somebody to find a lost child — never, no payment. All things being equal, if this were so, ministers and doctors should not accept money. Should they not represent God and serve humanity free of charge?

There was a tradition in my family that women were always very supportive, loyal, caring, protective, and sacrificing. I emulated my mother for all of my young womanhood.

Yet, I, too, needed support. I need to feel a supportive presence radiating from my family and from my friends. I need encouragement. ESP requires that and it requires a feeling of security.

I learned that my relationship must be that of equals each playing his or her role, each supportive of the other.

There have been times of disillusionment, times when I have decided never again to concentrate on ESP. They were bad times. I felt parapsychology was a futile venture, that I should be using my time and energy for more socially acceptable things; my music perhaps, or my long-desired college degree. But my friends rallied behind me and urged me to continue. Without their help and encouragement I could not have continued.

Final Psychic Thoughts

I did not wish to be known as psychic. I wanted only to be a part of parapsychological research. Because of my role in research — that of the subject, it seems that I cannot have one without the other. To admit a belief in ESP exposes one to severe criticism from many people. I have chosen to ignore such critics. I set about my personal studies in a deliberate attempt to understand this puzzling phenomena. ESP does not happen to me. I do it, that is the difference. I have often compared it to turning on a radio. I have attempted to use my ESP abilities in many different ways and in many different situations. In the years ahead, I will be cooperating in a long range research program concerning the role of the psychic sensitive in police work. This work is being done by a leading mid-western university. This is the type of challenge I always will find time to accept. I welcome it. What began as a mystery in my life remains a mystery. It was first of all a game that became an intellectual exercise for me; baffling, disappointing at times, but always intriguing. I learned much. I spoke everywhere — from the conservative campuses of New England to the New School for Social Research in New York City. I lectured before doctors, lawyers, teachers, scientists, students and civil engineers: for every civic organization one can imagine and for many church groups.

In the process, through the years I discovered that the level of one's educational background is not a factor in a belief or disbelief in the validity of ESP. Some PhD's believe it is so, and some do not. The same is true of the medical profession or the blue collar worker. This is best illustrated by the words of a psychology professor who said to me, "I wouldn't believe it even if you proved it to me." And in the opposite vein, the response of a world-famous radio astronomer, whom I met at California Institute of Technology: "Of course I accept it. My wife has ESP. I've observed it in my children. Some day they will study it in depth."

Much of the public still clings to its cherished beliefs in the ancient folklore. The study of parapsychology is constantly attacked as being non-rational and statistically unscientific. What is, then, the proper attitude toward this controversial subject? I would say, an unbiased non-judgmental one, taking a middle of the road approach, being neither a rigid skeptic nor a gullible believer. There is a saying in the space industry among those trained scientists who monitor the strange sounds from outer space with their incredibly sophisticated instruments, "There is a signal in the noise." In all the clamor about ESP and psychic phenomena there is also a signal trying to get through. Perhaps not in our lifetime, but someday, we shall come to understand it.

Appendix of Documents

In the process of researching and documenting specific and unusual major cases involving Shirley Harrison's acute and unique psychic abilities, the authors have tried to maintain as great a degree of accuracy as possible in this book.

In order to double check the accuracy of information provided by various key sources, the final manuscript was provided for review to each of the people involved. That verification is contained in this appendix.

These signed letters and approvals are on file at Guy Gannett Books, Portland, Maine. What follows are typeset copies of this material.

* * * *

Zelda R. Suplee
Consultant

Dec. 6, 1980

TO WHOM IT CONCERNS:

This will attest to the fact that I was a guest in the apartment of William O. Erwin, Ph.D. on West 13th Street, New York City, at the time when Mrs. Shirley Harrison, then residing in Saco, Maine, gave the following demonstration of her extraordinary psychic ability:

She was using the ouija-board method of obtaining information through unexplainable channels. After a while she said to the group watching her, "Ask me a question." Dr. Erwin then asked, "Where will the Boston Strangler strike next?"

After a few minutes Shirley Harrison reported, "A nurse in an apartment on Charles Street (or it may have been South Street, Boston) near a fire station." Naturally we were all startled and discussed what should be done with this information. Dr. Erwin then called Jess Stearn, the journalist involved in psychic research and author of books on the subject.

Months later I learned that the next victim was a young woman who had just moved into a first floor apartment just vacated by a nurse. The apartment was located near the firehouse as mentioned.

I also recall the account of Shirley Harrison's following the trail, through psychic sensitivity, of a man who had kidnapped his son who had been in his wife's custody. Despite the passage of time, some of the details are still clear in my mind: taking the boy cross country, southern route, placing him in an orphanage or convent temporarily, buying new sneakers, a new car — either sneakers or car were red — and eventually arriving in California.

Many other instances of Shirley Harrison's ability come to mind: diagnoses for physicians, locating remains of a person found in a quarry after 20 years, etc. etc.

SUBSCRIBED AND SWORN TO BEFORE ME
This 8th Day of Dec., 1980
/s/ June E. Iversen
Notary Public - California

OFFICIAL SEAL
JUNE E. IVERSEN
Notary Public - California
Los Angeles County
My comm. expires JULY 29, 1983.

/s/ Zelda R. Suplee

I am glad to attest to the accuracy of the above statements.

/s/ William O. Erwin Ph.D.

*   *   *   *

September 22, 1967

Dr. Thelma Moss
Neuropsychiatric Institute
U.C.L.A.
Los Angeles, California 90024

Dear Doctor Moss:

I first met Mrs. Shirley D. Harrison in April of 1965 when Mr. Charles Sanford of WGAN-TV here in Portland and I picked her up to bring her to the studio for a half hour un-rehearsed appearance on our station.

It was completely ad-lib. During the program she mentioned that she could foresee some heavy aerial bombing of North Viet Nam which, at that time, of course the U. S. was not doing.

As an example of what she had done in the past, she traced the movements of a father who had kidnapped his son from the custody of the mother. She told of his buying new shoes for the boy and described the color and the place they had been bought. These things were later verified by news reports.

As the climax of this half hour television appearance, she was asked to identify an object. It was a piece of barbed wire which had been brought home by one of our top management officials from the Berlin wall. She immediately described it and correctly identified it.

The audience reaction to her appearance was immediate and continued. In fact I still get calls inquiring where Mrs. Harrison may be reached.

I hope that this brief outline of my one meeting with her will be helpful in your work.

I am

Very sincerely,

/s/ Harry W. Marble
WGAN-TV News
390 Congress St.

HWM/cm
cc: S. Harrison

*   *   *   *

July 11, 1968

Dr. Thelma Moss
Neuro Psychiatric Institute
UCLA
Los Angeles, California

Dear Dr. Moss:

I have been requested by Mrs. Shirley Harrison of Buxton, Maine, to write to you and acquaint you with an incident which occurred about three years ago.

On Christmas Day of 1965, a 13 year old newspaper boy disappeared while making his paper route collections. His body was not found until mid-May of the following year. In the month of February prior to his body being found, I had conversation with Mrs. Harrison and asked her if she had had any thoughts regarding the whereabouts of this young paper boy by the name of Cyrus Everett. She informed me at that time that she felt that he had met with violent death and his body was resting in a watery spot with a heavy branch or tree over him in a place called Cheney.

This young boy's body was found three months later in Cheney's Pond in a marshy area with a 673 pound log covering him. The Medical Examiner concluded that he had died from a blow on the head and his body had been placed under this heavy log.

This report has been given to the Maine State Police and they have had conversation with Mrs. Harrison on this subject and other incidents that have happened in the State.

Sincerely,

/s/ Linwood F. Ross

LFR:em

cc: Mrs. Harrison

I hope I did a satisfactory job expressing this incident.

*   *   *   *

BEACH PHARMACY
Robert D. St. Laurent, B.S., Reg. Pharm.

39 Old Orchard St.   Old Orchard Beach, Maine

9/15/1980

Dear Mrs. Cook,   (Shirley's former married name)

It was pleasant talking with you yesterday about the book you are writing.

This letter is to confirm the fact that I related my paranormal experiences to you, these statements are accurate and true to the best of my knowledge and much of this incidence was in fact, witnessed.

I welcome any further questions and want to tell you to feel free to use any of the matter recorded on the tape made at said meeting in your book.

Respectfully,

/s/ Robert D. St. Laurent

*   *   *   *

PUBLICOVER
SECURITY SERVICE, INC.
367 St. John Street
Portland, Maine 04102
207-773-3736

September 18, 1980

Mr. Lynn Franklin
Route 2
Box 100
Sebago Lake, Maine 04075

Dear Lynn:

This letter will serve to confirm our conversation regarding
Mrs. Shirley Harrison Cook.

I have collaborated with Mrs. Cook during an investigation I
was conducting into the recovery of some missing jewelry. I
had given Mrs. Cook a brief discription of the circumstances
surrounding the case.

In a subsequent conversation with Mrs. Cook, she listed eight
items of jewelry. My original list consisted of five items.

I received a call from one of the principals in the case before
I had an opportunity to talk with him about my conversation
with Mrs. Cook. He called me to report an item of jewelry
that had turned up missing. The item he described was on the
list Mrs. Cook had given to me. The description of the item
matched an item Mrs. Cook had described to me which had
not been on my original list.

I look at everything and everybody sceptically, it's my habit.
Nothing is ever 100%. So that after she called me back — and
she had not been well. There was a lapse of some time — I
went to my files and looked up the information I had given
her. It was a letter. Some of the feedback I got from her
could have been derived from the information in the letter.

But the items she added to the list did not come from me. I had not described the companion or the property although I told her they existed. Her descriptions could not have come from me. I wanted to see whether she had not rehashed my information and given it back to me. She didn't. In my business we take certain information and come up with possibilities. I don't think she could have done that. She did not talk in generalities. She was definite and accurate, specific items and locations and personal characteristics.

I look forward to working with Mrs. Cook again. Certain information she had given me during my investigation was confirmed. The case is still under investigation and perhaps the remainder of the information will be certified.

Sincerely,

/s/ Bruce Albert Publicover
President

* * * *

GUY GANNETT PUBLISHING CO.

Book Division   Portland, Maine 04104
Allan A. Swenson, *Director*   (207) 775-5811, Ext. 327

Date: May 20, 1981

I have read the manuscript chapter of Psychic Search entitled Vanished, and it is a true and accurate account of my involvement in that case with Shirley Harrison to the best of my knowledge. I authorize use of this information and material in the forthcoming book, The Psychic Search, which is the story of Shirley Harrison.

/s/ Robert D. St. Laurent

Name: Robert D. St. Laurent

Witness: Dwight W. Berry

* * * *

GUY GANNETT PUBLISHING CO.

Book Division   Portland, Maine 04104
Allan A. Swenson, *Director*   (207) 775-5811, Ext. 327

Date: May 19, 1981

I have read the manuscript chapter of Psychic Search entitled The Diamond Solitaire, and it is a true and accurate account of my involvement in that case with Shirley Harrison to the best of my knowledge. I authorize use of this information and material in the forthcoming book, The Psychic Search, which is the story of Shirley Harrison.

/s/ Bruce A. Publicover

Name: Bruce A. Publicover

Witness: Marilyn Harris

*   *   *   *

GUY GANNETT PUBLISHING CO.

Book Division   Portland, Maine 04104
Allan A. Swenson, *Director*   (207) 775-5811, Ext. 327

Date: May 19, 1981

I have read the manuscript chapter of Psychic Search entitled Lost Aircraft, and it is a true and accurate account of my involvement in that case with Shirley Harrison to the best of my knowledge. I authorize use of this information and material in the forthcoming book, The Psychic Search, which is the story of Shirley Harrison.

/s/ Ernest L. Bracy

Name: Ernest L. Bracy

Witness: Floyd W. Lovejoy Jr.

*   *   *   *